Back to Learning

How research-based classroom instruction can make the impossible possible

Les Parsons

Pembroke Publishers Limited

Dedication

As always, to Susan: for her insights, encouragement, and support

© 2012 Pembroke Publishers
538 Hood Road
Markham, Ontario, Canada L3R 3K9
www.pembrokepublishers.com

Distributed in the U.S. by Stenhouse Publishers
480 Congress Street
Portland, ME 04101
www.stenhouse.com

We acknowledge the financial support of the Government of Canada through the Book Publishing Industry Development Program (BPIDP) for our publishing activities.

We acknowledge the assistance of the Government of Ontario through the Ontario Media Development Corporation's Ontario Book Initiative.

Library and Archives Canada Cataloguing in Publication

Parsons, Les,
    Back to learning : how research-based classroom instruction can make the impossible possible / Les Parsons.

Includes bibliographical references and index.

Issued also in electronic format.

ISBN 978-1-55138-281-4

    1. Effective teaching. 2. Classroom management. I. Title. II. Title: How research-based classroom instruction can make the impossible possible.

LB1025.3.P366 2012   371.102   C2012-903943-8

eBook format ISBN 978-1-55138-842-7

Editor: Kat Mototsune
Cover Design: John Zehethofer
Typesetting: Jay Tee Graphics Ltd.

Printed and bound in Canada
9 8 7 6 5 4 3 2 1

FSC
www.fsc.org
MIX
Paper from
responsible sources
FSC® C004071

CONTENTS

Doing What's Necessary

Teachers are already doing what's necessary—and designing, presenting, and marking lessons is merely the tip of the iceberg. Maintaining their balance against a tsunami of daily administrative, supervisory, extra-curricular, and communicative/collaborative tasks keeps them constantly in survival mode. When formal standardized testing or reporting to parents are added to teachers' duties, schools begin to shudder, steam, and hiccup like overheated leaky-valve engines.

Unfortunately, teachers are further handicapped in their efforts by shifts in the current educational climate. Teachers are discovering a troublesome trend in students' attitudes toward and approach to schooling, along with a relentless push by parents and school administrators to ensure that students achieve a standard expected by their parents. Newspapers constantly expose the scandalous levels of bullying in schools and no one seems to have a solution. Technological advances keep teachers on the defensive; the Internet revolution has left many teachers wondering about their relevance in the computer age and searching for ways to cope.

Far from being assured in and empowered by their own expertise and driven by professional commitment, many teachers feel confused, frustrated, and disenfranchised in the current educational climate. The research-based practice they encounter in their training is immediately subsumed by the realities of the workplace. What, when, and how they teach, and with what materials, are usually prescribed. How they evaluate learning and report to parents is also prescribed. Teachers quickly learn to do as they are told and to teach in the manner of their immediate peers.

Dramatic and permanent change in any of these issues seems unattainable. But teachers can alleviate the almost unbearable pressures of doing what's necessary by doing what's possible. A return to research-based practice will allow teachers to fulfil their necessary duties and, at the same time, regain their status as professionals. They need to base whatever they do in their classrooms on the best ways to teach and the most effective ways to learn. Empowered by knowledge, they can help shape a new direction and mandate for our schools.

But it's often difficult discovering the best ways to teach and the most effective ways to learn. Outdated or badly interpreted research has a way of becoming "truth." Over time, a huge body of this common wisdom infuses the profession, becoming the basis for its mandates and practices. It is seldom questioned, even when research and the reality of the teaching experience disprove those beliefs and methods. As a result, the methodology in schools can be an unsettling mix of misconceptions and assumptions with reality- and research-based practice.

See page 26 for answers to questionnaire.

Misconception or Research-Based Reality?

Read through the statements about learning and teaching, and decide which ones are misconceptions (M) and which ones represent practice based on how research reflects the reality of teaching (R).

1. Children praised for their intelligence are less successful at school tasks than those students praised for their effort.   M or R?
2. Boys are better with math and science than girls.   M or R?
3. Girls read and write earlier and more easily than boys.   M or R?
4. Boys need an activity-based curriculum, while girls thrive in a more structured text-based environment.   M or R?
5. Since boys lag behind girls in early education, boys-only schools give them a fair chance to compete among themselves and develop positive self-esteem.   M or R?
6. Since girls are math-challenged, they should learn in separate classes with a math-focused curriculum.   M or R?
7. Teachers need to devise right-brain or left-brain activities for different students with different learning styles.   M or R?
8. Teachers should employ a variety of aids and programs to help students access and develop the 90% of their brain they never use.   M or R?
9. Children born in January, February, or March will generally be significantly more developmentally mature than their younger peers.   M or R?
10. The more some children are selected out of a group, streamed, and given differentiated instructional experience, the more likely it is that they will carry that initial advantage on through their school life.   M or R?
11. Older students, such as teens, don't require the same kind of individualization that younger students do.   M or R?
12. Cooperative learning leads to increased higher-level thinking skills.   M or R?
13. Children streamed (i.e., grouped) for reading according to ability and kept in those groups over an extended period generally achieve higher reading scores.   M or R?
14. High-stakes standardized testing produces results at the expense of education.   M or R?
15. Grade inflation in our current schools is a myth.   M or R?
16. Functional illiteracy in both the United States and Canada is about 42% of the population.   M or R?

For a window into how confusing curricular beliefs can be, try the questionnaire above. Chapter 1, Doing What's Possible, will clear up any confusion about these statements and supply a research-based foundation for change. As with any change process, however, it's difficult to know where to start. In the midst of their crisis-filled days and inundated by the demands of their many responsibilities, teachers have a hard time maintaining a clear professional perspective. Focused as they are on a never-ending stand of trees, they can easily lose sight of the forest. What they need are a few basic principles to serve as the foundation for their teaching and the criteria against which any innovation should be judged.

Imagine, then, how a teacher's mind set might be revolutionized and the curricular dialogue changed if these three simple, fundamental laws of teaching were always followed:

The Three Laws of Teaching

1. Teachers must keep their students physically and emotionally safe;
2. Teachers must offer their students interesting and stimulating learning activities;
3. Teachers must keep their students feeling good about how they're learning.

Simple rules, such as these, would provide a litmus test for classroom teachers to apply to all their professional actions. As professionals, they would be required to resolve any dissonance between what they are told to do by their superiors and the rules that govern their classroom lives.

Teachers could use the three laws to better implement what they learn from current research to safeguard their students' self-esteem and individualize their classroom programs. They would immediately understand that tackling the corrosive issue of bullying must assume top priority in their classrooms and schools. As teachers struggle to define their role in the electronic age, the three laws of teaching can also transform how they look at and operate within the digital universe. Finally, the three laws can also serve as a springboard into the kinds of changes that classrooms of the future will certainly require.

1

Doing What's Possible

See the questionnaire on page 6 to assess the assumptions at play in decisions on teaching practice.

When you don't have control over what you do and how you go about doing it, it's difficult to know when and where your professionalism as a teacher comes into play. When politicians, parents, and board and school administrators determine what the curriculum should be, the methodology used to implement it, and the assessment tools used to evaluate it, teachers can tend to feel more like reluctant hired hands than independent self-reliant professionals. When school boards insist on wiring all aspects of curriculum into computer technology, for example, or a teacher's or school's effectiveness is decided through standardized testing scores, teachers never have the opportunity to think through for themselves where they stand on these issues or how to adapt these demands to their own beliefs about their professional responsibilities.

When teachers need to find ways to knit the necessary and the possible together, research can lead the way. Sometimes what teachers think they're doing and what they're actually doing are two very different things. A case in point is the issue of developing positive self-esteem. No one questions the importance of keeping students feeling good about how they are learning and the work they do. The third law of teaching demands it. The problem, however, is the way teachers and parents have gone about trying to raise self-esteem. As the pressure to achieve higher and higher scores increases, children are becoming less and less able to cope with the stress, mainly because more and more teachers and parents are burying students' initiative under an avalanche of undeserved praise. Self-esteem can all too easily be transmuted into a sense of entitlement.

A False Sense of Entitlement

As any teacher will attest, a sea change has occurred in how parents perceive their children and, subsequently, how those children perceive themselves. This change in perception has eroded the authority of teachers and undermined their expertise. Parents have raised their children to believe that each and every one of them is special, and therefore entitled to the kinds of marks and success in school that special children deserve.

This belief is unreasonable, untenable, and inimical to a healthy learning/teaching environment—but it's now a fact of life in many classrooms. That's why, from the primary grades to university, a grade of *A* has now become the new *B*: in 2011, for example, 43% of all college grades were *A* (*Harper's*, October 2011). The culprit is a misunderstanding and misapplication of a core learning/teaching concept. And many teachers are as culpable as parents.

We have all sorts of reasoning chains in education that inform what we do and how we go about doing it. One such chain cascades down from the concept of risk-taking. If students can internalize an understanding that mistakes or approximations are a positive and essential component of the learning process, they derive the freedom to experiment, explore the unknown, or try something new without unduly worrying about failing or being wrong. We then reasoned that a confident student necessarily takes on more risks than an apprehensive or timid student. Since confident students are self-assured and assertive, we needed only to find ways to build self-esteem in order to facilitate learning.

Following that logic, teachers and parents set about to build and protect students' self-esteem with a constant stream of praise and encouragement, regardless of achievement.

Tell them how smart they are and how well they're doing and students will blossom—or so we thought. The corollary stated that direct criticism should be avoided at all costs: criticism tears down self-esteem, and low self-esteem negates learning.

As a result, our children have been reared in a culture of narcissism that centres on the belief that they are all entitled to everything. In *Empire of Illusion*, Chris Hedges articulates the misguided conviction that "all of us, by tapping into our inner reserves of personal will and undiscovered talent, by visualizing what we want, can achieve, and deserve to achieve, happiness, fame, and success" (Hedges, 2009: 27).

As far as our understanding of self-esteem is concerned, it turns out we've had it all wrong. In *NurtureShock*, Po Bronson and Ashley Merryman survey research on the issue and offer convincing arguments that our logical pursuit of students' self-esteem is inherently flawed (Po & Merryman, 2009). Children praised for their intelligence, for example, are *less* successful at school tasks than children praised for their effort. Children who have been told they're smart expect that they will automatically know how to do something. Since they've seen their teachers time and time again exhorting students who have academic difficulties to "keep trying," they've also come to the conclusion that those who aren't smart have to work at everything.

As a consequence, so-called smart students have no effective way of responding to failure. When presented with problems whose solutions aren't readily apparent, they either give up or find some rationale for avoiding the task. From their point of view, if they expend more effort, they are just proving that they aren't as smart as they are supposed to be. Students praised for their effort, on the other hand, redouble their endeavors to find some way to complete a difficult task.

Regardless of gender, socio-economic class, or age, students praised for effort over intelligence dramatically improve their success at school tasks. In fact, a recent study of college students discovered that esteem-building with students who were close to failure produced even *lower* grades.

Rethinking the Use of Praise

The issue of praise is a double-edged sword. Praise has to be credible to be effective. In the single-minded pursuit of positive self-esteem, parents and teachers are often guilty of bestowing unwarranted praise on students. Too many parents find themselves so vicariously enmeshed in their offspring's development that criticizing their children amounts to criticizing themselves. Their excessive and disproportionate praise leads their children to an overly inflated and fragile opinion of their abilities that, again, tends to crash when they're confronted with failure.

Teachers are equally guilty of undermining their students' success with undeserved and insincere praise. Students quickly catch on to the behavior and think that the disingenuous teacher actually has little faith in their abilities; once a teacher's use of praise comes under question, even sincere praise is discounted. A teacher's goal is to keep students feeling good about themselves in the pursuit of learning. Insincere or superficial praise can actually interfere with that process.

We're only now realizing the difference between a healthy self-esteem, based on real achievement and honest feedback, and an artificially created self-esteem that is based on mere participation and uncritical praise. When parents or teachers constantly praise children for everything they do, no matter how routine, prosaic, or unsuccessful, the children develop a false sense of status and privilege; they see themselves as exceptional, unique, and entitled. Even "healthy self-esteem can quickly morph into an inflated view of oneself—a self-absorption and sense of entitlement that looks a lot like narcissism" (Gottlieb, 2011: 72).

This use of excessive praise escalates the negative outcomes: overly praised students become afraid to take risks or commit to a task in case they fail. Alarmingly, they tend to be consumed with maintaining their self-image to the extent that they focus totally on marks, exhibit highly competitive natures, and will lie, cheat, and belittle others in their attempts to merit the immoderate praise they're used to receiving. In a well-meaning but flawed approach to the third law of teaching, teachers ironically expose students to emotional harm by violating the first law.

Parents and teachers can aggravate the situation by inculcating a sense that mistakes are bad and poor grades represent failure. Besides depriving children of the opportunity to learn from their experiences, they exacerbate the children's insecurities by predicting that they will "do better next time." The struggle to immerse students in interesting and stimulating activities, as decreed by the second law of teaching, is effectively sabotaged when students are afraid to take advantage of new learning experiences.

Real risk-taking is crucial to effective learning. By handicapping students with an artificial and fragile sense of themselves and their abilities, well-meaning parents and teachers are actually creating barriers to risk-taking. With the educational environment stressed to the breaking point and ill-equipped to serve the needs of a disparate student population, students of all ages need to take risks more than ever before when, in reality, they are being taught to do the opposite.

A Return to Risk-taking

The cure is simple: honesty. Students deserve respect, compassion, and understanding. They also deserve honest feedback. With deference to their age, experience, capabilities, and feelings, all students can benefit from specific, genuine interest in their work and focused, explicit recommendations for improvement. This kind of interaction with students occurs naturally when teachers are able to

The Three Laws of Teaching

1. Teachers must keep their students physically and emotionally safe.
2. Teachers must offer their students interesting and stimulating learning activities.
3. Teachers must keep their students feeling good about how they're learning.

distinguish among their various roles in the classroom. The teacher as mentor can encourage change in ways that the teacher as supervisor or evaluator can't.

As mentor, a teacher needs to become personally involved in a child's individual struggle to achieve. Automatic and blanket praise for mere participation, as we've seen, has far-reaching negative consequences. If primary children, for example, are told over and over how wonderful their paintings or stories are, they lose perspective on the development of their skills and the purposes of communication.

On the other hand, if primary students are asked to describe their paintings or read their stories, teachers can use the content as a jumping-off point for discussion. Teachers might choose to inquire about the motivation for the work, ask which component of the work the student is especially proud of, and then indicate an aspect of the work that the teacher found particularly interesting or skilfully completed. The discussion can end with a suggestion of an area that the student might try to improve or expand on with the next attempt in that medium.

As students mature, they benefit even more from seeing teachers as participants themselves in experimenting with language and using their own mode of expression as a way to unlock meaning. As mentors, teachers can demonstrate or model the process of inquiring into all aspects of language development. They can present reading, writing, or discussion, for instance, as multifaceted open-ended activities in which adults and students take part for a variety of reasons and in a variety of ways across the curriculum. As directed by their students' needs, teachers can maintain a continuing dialogue with their protégés, supporting, advising, and guiding as necessary.

Obviously, students understand that their teacher is also assessing the quality of their efforts and that he or she will be filling out a report card that assigns a grade to their performance. At the same time, the effective teacher has instilled a belief that all students can and should improve: the gifted writers can't expect an automatic *A* based solely on their natural ability; the students struggling to master addition of fractions know they will be rewarded for improvement based on effort; and all students realize they are important participants in a community of learners. Maintaining a balance among the three laws is crucial: developing healthy self-esteem about themselves can never succeed in isolation from the other two laws.

Differentiating Instruction

See pages 18–22 for more on the difference between individualized and differentiated instruction.

One sure-fire way to raise students' self-esteem is by individualizing a program's content, pace, and methods of evaluation. That approach should make it easier for teachers to give all students interesting and stimulating things to do; individualized evaluation should keep students feeling good about themselves and what they were doing and achieving. All three laws are satisfied and learning is maximized.

The obvious problem with this theoretical solution is that our current curricular focus is on everyone learning the same thing, at the same time, in the same way, and being judged by the same tests. By the same token, a standardized approach leads to the dilemma described in the following fable.

The Animal School: A Fable

Once upon a time, the animals decided they must do something heroic to meet the problems of a "new world," so they organized a school. They adopted an activity curriculum consisting of running, climbing, swimming, and flying. To make it easier to administer the curriculum, all the animals took all the subjects.

The duck was excellent in swimming—in fact, better than his instructor. But he made only passing grades in flying and was very poor in running. Since he was slow in running, he had to stay after school and also drop swimming in order to practice running. This was kept up until his webbed feet were badly worn and he was only average in swimming. But average was acceptable in school, so nobody worried about that, except the duck.

The rabbit started at the top of the class in running but had a nervous breakdown because of the amount of makeup work in swimming.

The squirrel was excellent in climbing until she developed frustration in the flying class, where her teachers made her go from the ground up instead of the top of the tree down. She also developed tendonitis from overexertion, and then got a C in climbing and a D in running.

The eagle was a problem child and was disciplined severely. In the climbing class, he beat all the others to the top of the tree—but insisted on his own way of getting there.

At the end of the year, an abnormal eel that could swim exceedingly well, and also run, climb, and fly a little, had the highest average and was valedictorian.

The prairie dogs stayed out of school and fought the tax levy because the administration would not add digging and burrowing to the curriculum. They apprenticed their children to a badger and later joined the groundhogs and gophers to start a successful private school.

This fable was written by George Reavis when he was the Assistant Superintendent of the Cincinnati Public Schools in the 1940s. Then, as now, individualizing instruction was a thorny problem.

Certainly, "The Animal School" forces us to reflect on the need to individualize curriculum and evaluation to meet the needs of all our students, to be wary of a one-size-fits-all approach to both, and to consider the inherent difficulties involved in developing a fair, effective, and equitable approach to students with special needs.

Teaching to Gender

Instead of individualization, however, the trend in North American schools is toward streaming and differentiated instruction. For example, many teachers believe that students encounter certain kinds of problems in school because of their gender. Boys are better with math and science than girls; girls read and write earlier and more easily than boys. Boys need an activity-based curriculum, while girls thrive in a more structured text-based environment.

Since private schools have been siphoning students from the public systems with specialized instruction, North American public schools have increasingly attempted to compete by fracturing their egalitarian model and creating *boutique* schools. One type of boutique school insists on separating girls and boys for instruction.

If teachers believe that girls and boys learn differently and that each possesses an inherent learning handicap, that belief influences their methodology. Such a teacher in a gender-specific classroom will be looking for specific learning/ teaching methods designed for that gender alone. Such a teacher in a heterogeneous classroom will be on the lookout for learning difficulties based on a student's gender and ways to remediate the problem. More to the point, such teachers can expect boys and girls to have difficulty with certain types of tasks *because they are boys and girls*, and maintaining positive self-esteem in these situations is made more difficult by the belief that each gender possesses inherent weaknesses.

Research into this issue, however, presents a totally different picture from the common and prevailing wisdom. The current craze for gender-specific schools is actually based on a number of common misconceptions about the differences in how boys and girls learn. Since boys and girls possess qualitatively different brains, the argument goes, they naturally need to be taught in different ways. Since boys lag behind girls in early education, why not create boys-only schools to give them a fair chance to compete among themselves and develop positive self-esteem? Since girls are math-challenged, why not put them in separate classes with a math-focused curriculum?

Of course, religious schools sometimes separate boys and girls for religious reasons. For other schools, what does research say about placing boys and girls in separate classes? If men are from Mars and women are from Venus, and their brains are significantly different, then that kind of selection criteria might make some sense. Here on Earth, however, the science disclaims the practice.

MRI studies show that there are no essential differences between male and female brains. As well, many scientists now believe that, in the nature/nurture tandem, nurture is responsible for 80% of the brain's development. Social factors—such as how you perceive your own ability, how others perceive your ability, the amount and kinds of experiences and opportunities you receive, as well as diet, exercise, and health care—determine how your brain develops, regardless of gender. (Mitchell, 2009)

Neurobiologist Dr. Lise Eliot has discovered little evidence of gender differences in the developing brain (Eliot, 2009). Whatever small innate differences there might be are amplified over time by parents, teachers, and social immersion into a proscribed male or female culture. Common wisdom, for example, says that girls learn to speak much earlier than boys; in reality, the average difference is one month.

The belief that girls and boys have different-sized brains is another fallacy that derives from extrapolating a misperception about adult brains. At one time, people believed that there was a difference between adult men's and women's corpus callosums. Study after study has shown the opposite. The only difference is in average size, a fact that follows from the proportions of body size. Girls' brains, therefore, are no smaller than the brains of boys the same size.

In an important recent study, professors Jonathan Kane and Janet Metz (2012) analyzed data on math performances from 52 countries, including elite competitions, such as the International Mathematical Olympiad. They determined that any difference in math ability in males and females "can't be biologically innate" and that any difference in performance reflects social and cultural factors.

Regarding the question of developing separate schools or classrooms for boys and girls, Dr. Eliot declared that "the idea that the process of learning how to read or do arithmetic is fundamentally different for boys and girls is wrong and even dangerous." She went on to say that "the largest body of data from many countries—Canada, the U.S., Britain, Australia—suggests boys do not benefit from single-gender education compared with co-ed." (Eliot, 2009).

Differentiated instruction based on gender interferes with the proper functioning of the three laws. Teachers can, instead, offer all students access to interesting and stimulating activities regardless of gender, refute the idea that either gender is inferior or superior to the other, and keep students feeling good about themselves as gender-blind learners. Teachers also have to accept that attributing proficiencies or difficulties in any subject area to a difference in gender is erroneous. If a boy is a reluctant reader, it's not because he's a boy; if a girl is having difficulty with math, it's not because she's a girl. The research-based teacher rejects such simplistic excuses and delves into the real reasons behind an individual's success or failure. Students are simply individuals with individual brains—and therein lies another tale.

The Individualized Brain

Common beliefs about how the brain operates inform all aspects of schooling. Accepted practice in classrooms, for example, requires practitioners to teach to the different hemispheres of the brain; teachers commonly devise right-brain or left-brain activities for different students with different learning styles. Many teachers also employ a variety of aids and programs to help students access and develop the 90% of their brain we are told they never use. Parents and early childhood teachers attempt to create as much stimulation as possible for children's developing brains; the more children are stimulated, the better for their brains. And, of course, we've all heard that an individual's important learning is completed by the age of three.

But how many of these ingrained beliefs are actually supported by research and how many are merely flawed folklore? Science is fighting an uphill battle to clear the fog of accepted practice. Few teachers and fewer parents are aware that neuroscience is shattering some commonly held beliefs about children's brains and, in the process, sending education back to the future. At birth, for example, regardless of gender, race, socio-economic status, or where they live, children's brains are all about the same (Mitchell, 2009).

In a series on education for the *Toronto Star*, Alanna Mitchell dispelled a number of myths about the brain and how it functions. Some parents, for example, try to turn their baby's environment into an educational Disneyland, with flashcards adorning the house, drills on number facts, elaborate learning devices and games, and as many bells and whistles as they can find. They are reacting to the commonly held belief that the more you enrich a baby's environment, the smarter the baby will be; they're also concerned that, as accepted wisdom preaches, the human brain is fixed by the age of three.

Overstimulating babies, on the contrary, actually forces them to shut down and interferes with learning. Mitchell advocates immersing babies in a normal life: interacting with their parents, playing with other children, and encouraging them to explore on their own (Mitchell, 2009). And we now know that the brain grows and changes throughout an individual's lifetime and doesn't just stagnate from age three onwards.

Another commonly held belief states that we ordinarily use only 10% of our brains. Educational suppliers, of course, are ever ready to capitalize on this misguided information about the learning process. You can find any number of teaching aids and resource materials designed to engage the 90% of the brain that we never use. Neurobiologists, on the other hand, now understand that 100% of the brain is always active, even while sleeping.

Teachers were also told at one time that children are either left-brain or right-brain learners. For that reason, teachers have gone to great lengths to separate their teaching into left- and right-brain activities to accommodate all their students and the manner in which they learn. The only trouble with this approach is that both sides of the brain are integrated; neither side can operate independently. What we've also known for a long time is that a good program is a good program for anyone, regardless of ability, preferred learning style, gender, ethnicity, or any other artificial separation and grouping of children. One component that does seem to matter, however, is age.

Age Matters

Kindergarten teachers know that age matters. Describe a child underachieving or overachieving in Kindergarten and they will immediately ask when that child was born. They've learned from experience that children born in January, February, or March will generally be significantly more developmentally mature than their younger peers. These older, more mature children have a natural head start over other children. But educators and parents have come to believe that time will allow the younger children to catch up with their older counterparts. In the best of all schools in the best of all possible worlds, this belief might hold true. In the real world, catching up often doesn't happen.

The more some children are selected out of a group, streamed, and given differentiated instructional experience, the more likely it is that they will carry that initial advantage on through their school life (Gladwell, 2011). That initial selection, however, is often made on the basis of maturity, not ability—even though teachers will tell you otherwise.

Teachers, unfortunately, tend to confuse maturity with ability, a misleading perception that can have a profound cumulative effect. More mature children test higher than their younger counterparts. As a result of these results, they are placed in higher-ability groupings and given superior instruction. As students advance through the grades, the pattern is replicated time and again. Many younger children never catch up or are never recognized as having caught up.

In his book *Outliers*, Malcolm Gladwell illuminates this problem by citing research from economists Kelly Bedard and Elizabeth Dhuey. By comparing results from international testing with month of birth, they found that the oldest children in fourth grade scored between four and twelve percentile points higher than the youngest children. They also discovered that this advantage continued into college: members of the oldest group are almost 12% more likely to enter a four-year college.

Gladwell suggests that streaming all children from the beginning of school into three age groupings would solve this inequity by allowing students of the same age to compete against each other. One problem with this solution is that Gladwell seems to equate learning with competition; given our North American fanatical attraction to standardized testing, that conclusion is understandable.

More to the point, however, selecting students on the basis of age and then streaming them into different classes would inevitably lead to differentiated instruction: teachers would teach differently to the more mature children than to the less mature. In this model, selection, streaming, and differentiated instruction would simply lead to the same results: the oldest children getting all the breaks.

A much better, albeit more difficult-to-implement, model relies on individualizing instruction for all students, regardless of ability. Some educators seem to believe that older students, such as teens, don't require the same kind of individualization that younger students do—that's one reason why schools lower the pupil-to-teacher ratio in the primary grades at the expense of a higher pupil-to-teacher ratio in the later grades. But brain research teaches otherwise.

In their teens, students experience a major cerebral reorganization centred in the brain's frontal cortex, the area responsible for highest-level thinking and analysis. Abstract thinking, systems analysis, and goal-setting are burgeoning functions as teens follow their brain development into exploring who they are and trying to understand the world around them.

This outward movement merges innately with a need to develop social networks that allow teens to experience and learn from interactions with others. They learn best when they can follow their individual interests by deciding what they what to find out about and learning how to go about answering their own questions (Mitchell, 2009). The three laws of teaching can help teachers establish the kind of learning/teaching environment that suits how the brain learns: physically and emotionally secure, students can freely and confidently interact with others; individualizing the program allows students to follow their interests and, by definition, remain engaged in the program; and any kind of self-directed activity reinforces self-esteem, encourages independent inquiry, and maximizes learning.

The Classroom Divided

With declining enrolments a fact of life, more and more students are learning in split-grade classrooms. Although split-grade classrooms (e.g., Grades 4 and 5 with one teacher) are a long-standing fact of life, in many jurisdictions a few new wrinkles have been added to make this already-difficult practice an almost impossible challenge.

In the past, teachers who had to take responsibility for two grades in one classroom had some flexibility. They could teach one grade's history to both grades one year, for example, and switch the following year; they might integrate one aspect of the curriculum with another; they might focus on core skills regardless of content; and some jurisdictions even produced special blended programs especially for split-grade classrooms.

In many areas, these accommodations for split grades are no longer possible. To ensure uniformity within a school district, for example, teachers of split grades are often required to teach a different course of study to each grade. The courses of study are so different that no blending of grades is possible. Since all subjects are to be taught and evaluated separately, teachers of split grades are often handling two separate demanding curricula at the same time. Dropping enrolments and cutbacks to staffing mean an even greater proliferation of split grades. Principals have no choice but to organize their classrooms according to the staff they're given, and teachers cut corners here, there, and everywhere to cope with their impossible assignments.

At the same time, a lack of funding has forced cutbacks to special education programs. The traditional support for students who are two or more years behind their peers requires a formal assessment that may take a year or more to complete. While that process unfolds, these students remain in the regular classroom. As well, other students, who are encountering significant difficulties with learning but not enough to receive additional support, become the responsibility of the classroom teacher, whether or not those students are in a single-grade or split-grade classroom.

The classroom teacher then has the responsibility to plan, execute, evaluate, track, and report on an individual program that accommodates each student with specific learning disabilities. Special education classrooms were initially implemented precisely because classroom teachers struggled to effectively meet the needs of students with specific learning disabilities while, at the same time, maintaining a regular classroom program. Dealing with this added responsibility requires considerable ingenuity, especially for the many teachers already struggling with split-grade classrooms.

When special education students are integrated into a regular classroom program, teachers accommodate them with a variety of strategies. These students are often assigned fewer questions, given alternatives or more time to complete regular classroom assignments, offered more explicit direction and assistance during testing, or encouraged to take the work home for parents to collaborate on. The directive to classroom teachers from administrators is often to do whatever it takes to make sure the student receives a passing grade.

Not surprisingly, schools are turning to computer technology to assist overwhelmed teachers with special education. Many schools and school boards are also purchasing site licences for assistive reading and writing computer programs. These programs commonly contain such features as speech feedback in a document or on the web, talking dictionaries, word prediction, and audio file creation. These programs are designed to assist visually impaired students to gain access to both electronic and printed text by speaking aloud material that has been scanned or copied. They're also aimed at students with significant learning disabilities, such as dyslexia.

The first hurdle when using these types of programs is for the teacher and the students to learn the program themselves. The one-time tutorial process is often difficult and time-consuming. If parents intend to use the program at home, they also have to be taught it. The second obstacle is the nature of the programs themselves. They operate in a linear step-by-step fashion and often emphasize words in isolation and language as a rote-learning process. The danger lies in the temptation to use these programs with all students with any kind of learning difficulty or with all students regardless of their learning abilities. For most students, the best way to improve reading skills is by actually reading and the best way to improve writing skills is by actually writing.

A Return to All for One, One for All

One approach to individualizing instruction and maximizing learning seems counterintuitive: implement cooperative learning. Cooperative learning is the umbrella term for students collaborating through talk; this is the most powerful learning/teaching strategy yet developed. Through small-group activities, students interact with and learn from one another, in the process creating a potent problem-solving group dynamic. By collaborating on a regular basis in pairs and in groups of up to five or six, students can develop the interactive skills necessary to share and build on the foundation of each other's interests, backgrounds, experiences, and insights.

Cooperative learning, effective with all age groups and in all subject areas, has consistently produced the following benefits:

- Improved learning results, especially for average students and students at risk
- Higher academic achievement
- More effective problem-solving
- Increased higher-level thinking skills
- More positive attitudes toward subjects
- Greater motivation to learn

Equally important, cooperative learning strategies help students develop the process skills they need to become aware of and able to counter bias, discrimination, and bigotry of all kinds. Cooperative learning intrinsically follows the imperatives of the three laws of teaching. Cooperative learning also supports an intrinsic feature of what it means to be human. In a *Scientific American* article (June 2012), it is stated that "cooperation has been a driving force in the evolution of life on Earth from the beginning" and that cooperation has played as major a role as competition in human evolution.

With all this validation and all these benefits, why isn't cooperative learning an integral and daily component of classroom activity? Business leaders consistently rate group-processing skills as being highly desirable, and perceive a weakness in this area in their new hires. In the isolating environment of the electronic age, learning to navigate face-to-face talk-based collaboration neatly addresses one of the shortcomings of computer-based interactions. Research supports the approach, students need it, business wants it—yet cooperative learning remains a seldom-used and poorly understood learning/teaching strategy.

The primary reason, of course, lies in evaluation. When an evaluation system is based on competition, cooperation for the good of all is not only suspect but counterproductive. Why help someone else to a better grade when you are spending all your effort to be better than everyone else? The simple answer to that concern lies in rewarding students individually for their ability to apply group-processing skills. Students can still excel while helping to advance the goals of the group.

An effective set of cooperative learning strategies depends more on a set of specific processing skills than on any individual program. Students need to acquire and practice these skills to be able to apply them in any given situation. These skills invest a student with the awareness, knowledge, and ability both to cooperate with others in a fair, reasonable, and equitable manner, and to identify and resist anyone attempting to take over or subvert others in a group for their own purposes. They also equip students to adapt to any collaborative problem-solving situation and to interact effectively with others in their personal lives.

To be effective members of any group interaction, students need to become proficient with all of the following skills:

Sharing requires students to learn how to
- freely offer opinions, feelings, or special knowledge in an effort to further group process
- listen carefully to link what the group knows to what they know
- give facts and reasons to support opinions

Replying requires students to learn how to
- listen carefully so that they can ask clarifying questions or make clarifying statements

Another reason for the failure to implement cooperative learning is the confusion created by various formal programs, such as the Jigsaw Strategy developed by psychologist Elliot Aronson in the 1970s, the suspect but ever-popular brainstorming technique, or programs for developing social skills, such as Jeanne Gibbs' Tribes program.

- respond freely to other people's questions, interests, problems, and concerns
- make sure they share equally in the talking

Leading requires students to learn how to
- suggest ideas, other ways to solve problems, or new directions for the group to explore to keep the group headed in the right direction
- speak up without cutting off someone else or impeding the progress the group is making
- offer suggestions without dominating the group

Supporting requires students to learn how to
- help another group member have a turn to speak
- speak without cutting off another person or too abruptly changing the subject
- indicate by gesture, facial expression, or posture that they're interested in what is being said

Evaluating requires students to learn how to
- indicate whether or not they agree with ideas and decisions, and express reasons for taking a position
- consider how well the group is working and how they might help the group work even more effectively
- re-examine their opinions and decisions, and adjust them when someone else comes up with better ideas

Effective collaboration doesn't just happen. Students need direct instruction in the skills required of a productive group member. They need to become aware of the different roles in a group they will need to fulfil at various times and to be given opportunities to practice them. They also need to understand that they will be evaluated on how well they master the collaborative skill set.

For group discussions to be productive, students have to be taught how and when to share, reply, lead, and support during the course of a discussion, as well as how to constantly evaluate the group's progress to determine how best to maintain group integrity and efficiency. As the group advances toward a range of intellectual goals across the curriculum, individuals within the group also achieve maximum academic and social benefits (Parsons, 2005: 29–30). Inherently engaged and stimulated, both by the application of their problem-solving skills and the independence and interdependence promoted by the process, students reap the benefits of the three laws of teaching by essentially teaching themselves.

A Head Start for Everyone

A reason often advanced for developing gender-specific classrooms is that boys supposedly need a different kind of classroom environment. Boys are said to require more freedom of movement and choice as they learn and, in general, a more concrete and physical approach to learning. The problem here is in how a contemporary primary classroom is visualized. In this stereotype, the environment is teacher-centred and strictly controlled. Children are assigned to specific desks in rows or small groups of desks. They stay in these seats for the rest of the year. Little movement is required or allowed. The teacher stands at the head of the classroom and teaches lessons. After these lessons, the children are usually assigned paper-and-pencil tasks. Except for reading groups, children usually work at the same activity with the same resources and the same expectations. The teacher teaches the lesson, the children practice the learning, the learning is tested, and the teacher marks and records the results. In all cases, individuality is sacrificed for uniformity.

The trouble with this approach is that it's an extremely inefficient and ineffective way for anyone to learn, let alone young boys and girls. All children learn best when they are actively involved in the learning process, taking responsibility for and making decisions related to their own learning. They learn best, then, in a rich, varied, and stimulating environment constructed by a teacher following the three laws of teaching.

In such an environment, individually and in small flexible groups, children learn through reading, writing, observing, viewing, listening, discussing, and doing. The "doing" aspect of an activity-based program includes such activities as making, performing, calculating, experimenting, manipulating objects, and creating.

Just as important is the opportunity after each activity for participants to consciously reflect on and communicate what they thought about the nature of the learning experience. As children grow older, they can be urged to focus on their own patterns of thought and become aware of how and, for mature students, why they process experience in the singular way they do. (See Chapter 4, page XX.)

Primary children are not tiny adults. Their needs are specific to the way they are exploring the world and their place in that world; they need a specific kind of school environment to maximize their learning.

To understand this kind of learning/teaching environment, imagine a different kind of primary classroom:

To accommodate the needs of an activity-based child-centred program, the room itself is much larger than an ordinary classroom. The desks and small tables are flexibly grouped to provide a variety of work surfaces: children's books and other learning and personal items are kept in plastic bins arranged along one wall.

Along another wall are a number of bookracks with hundreds of fiction and nonfiction books, ranging from picture books to simple novels to dictionaries and thesauri. A rug and two comfortable chairs in this area satisfy the need for a meeting place for the daily read-alouds by the teacher, for individuals to read to the teacher, and for large-group activities.

An easel with lined chart paper (or an interactive white board) allows the teacher to create cooperative chart stories or for individual students to dictate stories to the teacher. You notice that the walls are filled with chart stories and that individuals are often guided to review and read from them.

Nearby, three computer stations provide opportunities for students to augment their time in the school's computer lab. Students use the computers for word processing, for reference, and to access a range of educational programs.

A number of activity stations are scattered around the room: one is a Lego station with a challenge to build a skyscraper; another is a play clay station where children are modelling dinosaurs after their latest science lesson; other children are working at a painting station, a puppet theatre, a crafts table, a sand table, and a water table, all focused by the teacher on themes and activities deriving from their studies and their own lives.

Some children are using math counters and other math manipulatives to help them with the day's arithmetic concepts, others are writing personal stories in their notebooks or practicing their printing, while others are lying on the floor flipping through picture books.

A busy, underlying hum provides a backdrop to the flow of purposeful movement. Children are talking, creating, and moving, absorbed and occupied by their assigned tasks.

Restoring the Focus on Learning and Language

The kind of activity-based child-centred classroom described here is an ideal learning environment, not just for boys but for everyone. All children flourish in a rich, varied, and stimulating classroom environment. This kind of environment is especially vital in the teaching of language. Language is an active, creative thinking process that, at any one time, incorporates aspects of listening, speaking, reading, writing, enacting, or representing. A single reading task, for example, can engage a student in a range of discussion and composing activities in a blended and recursive manner. From the point of view of the child, all aspects of language are intrinsically integrated. Making meaning is the key.

For children, language is a vital, natural, and purposeful activity. Through language, they construct their sense of reality by clarifying, discovering, assessing, reflecting on, resolving, and refining what they think and feel about experience. The more the basic elements of the language process are fragmented and isolated, the more language appears to be an artificial and arbitrary activity.

Too often, we still find the following discredited techniques in many primary classrooms:

- Children streamed (i.e., grouped) for reading according to ability and kept in those groups over an extended period
- Children reading for the purpose of answering questions or completing "busywork" from a workbook, with each exercise translated into testing for marks
- Children involved in round-robin reading (members of a group arbitrarily reading aloud one after another, often from the same story), with accurate word-calling the primary requirement
- Children restricted to a single basal reader or book
- Phonics instruction removed from the context of the student's actual reading experiences and, often, focused on a phonics workbook
- Words taught and tested in isolation

In an effective reading program, on the other hand, teachers build in time and opportunity to frequently and regularly read aloud to students. In such a reading program, students self-select reading material based on their interests and abilities, have time to read independently in class as opposed to answering written questions, and respond to their reading in personally significant ways,

Reading is an essential life skill and the foundation for success in school as students progress through the grades. Fluent readers can handle the text-based teaching of the later grades and can independently research the questions that their individual interests and curiosity pose. (An in-depth description of effective reading and writing practices for students of all ages is continued in Chapter 3, page 63.)

Cooperative Learning to Bridge the Divide

Implementing cooperative learning strategies is a proactive and organic way to tackle the challenges of split-grade classrooms and integrated special education. Cooperative learning is effective with all age groups and in all subject areas and produces improved learning results, *especially for average students and students at risk.* Other benefits include higher academic achievement, more effective problem-solving, increased higher-level thinking skills, and more-positive attitudes toward subjects. Regardless of whether the grade is split or if special education students have been integrated into the program, when students learn through small-group talk-based activities, the teacher is relieved of the task of being "the sage on the stage" and can instead observe, guide, remediate, and evaluate the learning on an individual basis. The teacher reading aloud, for example, is a simple but potent way to provide all students, regardless of reading ability, a common experience to enjoy, learn from, discuss, and analyze. At all grade levels, teachers need to frequently and regularly read aloud to students, especially nonfiction from content-area subjects, such as science or history.

The more a classroom program is individualized according to each student's background, interests, learning abilities, and pace of learning, the more successful that program will be. In English/language arts programs, students need to self-select reading material based on their interests and abilities, have time to read independently in class as opposed to answering written questions, and respond to their reading in personally significant ways, such as with response journals (see page 70). Again, the responsibility for individualizing curriculum is automatically placed on the student and not the teacher. In the same way, writing programs based on a writer's workshop model and incorporating meaningful student collaboration benefits all students regardless of their writing fluency and skill (see page 65).

At this point, however, the elephant in the room emerges: evaluation. In a very real sense, what teachers do in the classroom is predicated on the kind of testing a school or school board prescribes. Parents expect that teachers can assess children with scientific accuracy and predict their present and future educational needs. They believe that's what standardized testing produces. In response to those beliefs, most boards of education have instituted comprehensive systems of standardized testing. As standardized testing has proliferated, however, the validity of this type of testing has come under intense and critical scrutiny.

Standardized Testing and Learning Outcomes

Placed in the context of the three laws of teaching, standardized testing creates a stressful and uncertain learning/teaching environment, narrows and standardizes the curriculum, and explicitly turns learners into "winners" and "losers." Advocates for standardized testing, however, assert that the ends justify the means. At the heart of the hue and cry for standardized testing is the belief that standardized testing leads to improved learning outcomes. One of the leading advocates for standardized testing was Diane Ravitch, the education historian and assistant secretary of education in charge of the Office of Educational Research and Improvement for the administration of U.S. President George H.W. Bush. She was President George W. Bush's education "brain."

As part of the government, Ravitch believed that school reform should include accountability, high-stakes testing, data-driven decision making, choice, charter schools, privatization, deregulation, merit pay, and competition among schools.

Since leaving the government, however, she's had an astonishing change of heart and has recounted her conversion in her book, *The Death and Life of the Great American School System: How testing and choice are undermining education*. She now believes that the standardized testing mania is generating geysers of data with little relevance to the flow of knowledge. Measurable results have replaced education of children: punishment and rewards have replaced collaboration and professionalism.

While Ravitch's conversion and subsequent about-face on the issue of high-stakes testing is welcome, she's only now treading a well-travelled path. The case against such testing has been made over and over again. One critic of standardized testing has been journalist Alfie Cohn, who is among the most outspoken critics of education's single-minded focus on grades and test scores. Cohn published an eloquent and comprehensive rebuttal of the arguments in favor of high-stakes testing (Kohn, 2000).

In fact, researchers have discovered that high-stakes testing produces results at the expense of education. As low-performing students drop out, results improve; the curriculum narrows to the confines of the standardized tests; and subjects not included in standardized testing are neglected for test preparation. In 2005, for example, two-thirds of New York City's eighth-grade students were rated "below basic" in science. "Basic" is the lowest possible ranking. (Ravitch, 2010)

Standardized testing and test preparation, in fact, have even become daily activities in many New York City and Los Angeles Kindergarten classrooms. Teachers have reported spending between 20 and 30 minutes a day on test-related activities. In New York City, for example, Kindergarten children take a standardized test to determine whether they qualify for gifted programs, and children in Kindergarten and Grades 1 and 2 are tested as part of a school's performance evaluation (Association for Childhood Education International, 2009).

Of course, in the pressure-cooker atmosphere of high-stakes accountability, trends can be quickly adjusted. The National Center for Education Statistics in the U.S. estimates that, since 2005, 50% of American schools have lowered proficiency standards to inflate test scores. In New York City in 2007, for instance, 23% of elementary and middle students received an *A* grading; by 2009, 84% received an *A*.

High schools have followed suit. Grade inflation has eaten away at the integrity of high-school marks. A majority of applicants to university now have higher than 80% averages. Needless to say, too many students arrive at university unable to read fluently for meaning, write in a grammatically correct fashion, manage higher mathematics, or comprehend complex scientific concepts (Coates & Morrison, 2011: 34).

In another example of grade inflation, the province of Ontario yearly awards cash grants to high-school students with an average of 80% in their final year. About 50 years ago when the program was introduced, 3% to 5% of graduating students achieved this average: by 2010, 50% of graduating students had arrived at the 80% benchmark (Coates & Morrison, 2011: 183).

The Failure of Sanctions and Incentives

In spite of grade inflation, what happens when enough students don't meet the prescribed standards? In the United States, one-third of students meet the "proficiency" standard for reading; that means, of course, that two-thirds score below that level. The poison that lurks within that bitter pill is the fact that the No Child Left Behind (NCLB) law decreed that 100% of students must achieve a "proficiency" rating by 2014 or their schools would suffer the consequences. Sanctions would include school closures, the firing of teachers and principals, and privatization. Meanwhile, the U.S. Department of Education estimated that in 2011, 83% of U.S. public schools would fail under the standards of NCLB.

By 2012, President Obama officially acknowledged that the goals of NCLB were unattainable by offering states a way out of the law's toughest requirements. Most states lined up to submit their own federally approved plans as substitutes for NCLB.

Incentives are designed to get some people to do what other people want them to do. In education, marks have traditionally acted as the major incentive to stimulate learning. As well as an incentive for student improvement and a reward for student achievement, they also provide a window into student progress and an indication of how well a particular program or approach is working. But incentives don't always work the way they're intended to, especially when politicians dabble in education. Economists understand the difficulties involved in finding not only the right incentive but also the right degree of incentive. Politicians often have difficulty with these distinctions.

The United States is a strong proponent of high-stakes testing: the stakes are high because teachers and schools are held accountable for their students' results on standardized tests. On the surface, the concept seems reasonable. Even before President Bush's No Child Left Behind law mandated high-stakes testing in 2002, a number of states already rewarded individual schools for good results and sanctioned schools for poor results.

Typical sanctions for teachers with poorly performing students included official rebukes, loss of pay, or exclusion from promotion: teachers with high-performing students, on the other hand, could receive letters of commendation, pay raises or bonuses, and promotion. Poorly performing schools could have their funding slashed, their teachers placed on probation or fired, or the school closed and the teachers reassigned.

These kinds of pressures produce predictable courses of action. States often use their legislative powers to set their own standards, choose their own tests, and define "proficiency" as they find necessary; curriculum often turns into a mind-numbing succession of test preparation and low-level skill and drill exercises.

Many teachers, on the other hand, believe that the results of standardized testing are usually beyond their control. Although today's test-makers attempt to remove racial and gender bias from their tests, the correlation between achievement on these tests and socio-economic factors remains. Crudely put, the more money your parents make the better you will likely score on standardized tests. Attitudes toward and success with school in previous years also influence students' acceptance of and engagement with classroom programs, as do facility with the dominant language and experience with the jargon and procedures of the tests themselves.

Almost one-third of young people in the 9th grade fail to complete high school four years later; barely half of black and Hispanic students graduate on time with a regular diploma. And far too many of those who do complete high school lack the skills needed to succeed in the workplace. (Corporate Voices for Working Families, 2008)

In the meantime, standardized testing programs are failing to produce the results for which they're designed. Functional illiteracy in both the United States and Canada is about 42% of the population: that figure includes those who are illiterate, those who can't read well enough to fill out a job application, and those who are reading at a Grade 4 or 5 level. And that number is growing (Hedges, 2009: 44).

Answers to the questionnaire on page 6:

1. R
2. M
3. M
4. M
5. M
6. M
7. M
8. M
9. R
10. R
11. M
12. R
13. M
14. R
15. M
16. R

Evaluation has been called the tail that wags the educational dog. With the advent of high-stakes accountability, standardized testing is now the dog that wags the educational tail. It's also the fabricated Holy Grail that keeps schools chasing scores at the expense of learning. To understand where this obsession with marks will lead, simply look to South Korea. In 2010, 84% of high-school students, 50% of middle-school students, and 45% of elementary students attended private after-school tutoring academies called *hagwon*. *Hagwon* classes entail three to four hours of study above and beyond the regular school day and assignments, and children as young as three years old can be enrolled.

The focus of this type of schooling is rote learning—acquiring information by repetitive drill rather than understanding—and the goal is to develop grades that will give children access to the better universities. This relentless drive for better grades leads students into cram memorizing sessions that often last past midnight. The mania is so widespread that government has been forced to set curfews for these schools and offer rewards to anyone who will turn in an illegally operating academy (Li, 2011).

Hagwon offer a clear illustration of what can happen to teaching when the three laws of teaching are abandoned: learning devolves into a single-minded grind to arrive at an arbitrary number.

Getting Back to Good Programs

Bill Gates has said that any teaching you can't measure is useless.

But children are incredibly complex, interrelated networks of physical, emotional, and intellectual capacities, experiences, and learned behaviors, all of which change profoundly over time. A standardized test is a crude snapshot, at best, that can never measure or represent any child's learning condition. For that reason alone, teachers and parents must be aware of and responsive to the limitations of evaluation.

In education, we can observe some simple, specific natural behaviors and predict some rudimentary educative actions. A Kindergarten child, for instance, who experiences difficulty grouping concrete objects is not developmentally ready to begin pen-and-paper arithmetic computations; so the teacher devises further concrete grouping activities. On the other hand, that child's initial difficulty has no bearing on whether or not the child, when developmentally ready, will be able to efficiently add, subtract, multiply, or divide.

In the same way, a child who enjoys being read to, who is eager to read aloud favorite books she or he has memorized, and who repeatedly flips through storybooks, making up a story to suit the pictures, is probably ready to begin reading independently. Whether or not the child will develop into a fluent, efficient, lifelong reader is quite another matter.

The variables that determine such outcomes are too numerous, complex, and subtle to be accurately and reliably measured by any test we have now or that Bill Gates may devise in the future. Knowledgeable and experienced teachers, however, can identify tendencies and offer possibilities based on their day-to-day observations over a period of time. Conflict arises when parents and politicians demand sure things, and teachers can provide only best guesses.

With standardized testing being a way of life in most school boards, teachers need to satisfy the demands of standardized tests while, at the same time, maintaining their professional integrity. Students certainly need some basic preparation for standardized testing. Teachers need to familiarize students with the type and structure of standardized tests. Students also need run-throughs with similar tests under testing conditions to make the experience familiar and less intimidating. But this preparation should be secondary to the daily task of helping students acquire the skills and knowledge that will best prepare them for any kind of evaluation, including standardized testing.

The starting point for any teacher at any grade level is the challenge to create the best program possible within the constraints of prescriptive curricula and without making allowances for standardized testing. Fortunately, a good program is a good program is a good program. A student-centred, individualized, and activity-based elementary-school program, for example, benefits special-needs students, gifted students, students with English as a second language, as well as every other student.

The following chapters explore in detail what needs to be done to ensure the safe and secure learning/teaching environment that will allow good programs to flourish, to create the kinds of approaches that will inspire students in the digital age, and to return teachers to the best, time-proven, and most effective classroom practices.

2

Solving the Bullying Puzzle

The Three Laws of Teaching

1. Teachers must keep their students physically and emotionally safe.
2. Teachers must offer their students interesting and stimulating learning activities.
3. Teachers must keep their students feeling good about how they`re learning.

Bullying in schools strikes at the very heart of the learning/teaching process. Bullies inject fear and uncertainty into the school environment. Many students feel physically, emotionally, or socially threatened. They can't take full advantage of the interesting and stimulating things they're given to do; they can't even feel good about themselves. For these reasons, all three laws of teaching require teachers to make eradicating bullying their top priority.

Every school has anti-bullying policies. All schools have a variety of anti-bullying programs in place to ensure that bullying simply isn't a problem: the packaged, step-by-step lessons that every class receives once a week; the code of behavior that supposedly is strictly enforced; the fact that the peer-mediation program effectively takes care of any bullying; the special anti-bullying team that conducts intensive anti-bullying workshops for a week throughout the whole school; or the anti-bullying play written and performed by a neighboring high school's students and put on one afternoon in your school.

Every so often, though, a bullying incident among students occurs that is so horrific and unsettling it receives widespread attention in the media. That's when the public is informed about how bullying is a wide-spread, insidious, and deadly problem. That's also when school boards and their individual schools go into public-relations overdrive. We hear about the vigilance of the vast majority of teachers, the success of the various, anti-bullying programs, the existence of a "few bad apples" in an otherwise kind and nurturing school population, or the fact that this type of behavior happens only in "certain types of schools."

Research into school bullying paints a dramatically different picture. But in spite of consistent research findings that contradict the positive anecdotal reports from principals and other administrators, the public is reassured that the problem is well in hand. And schools go right back to functioning the way they always have, at least until the next deplorable incident happens to hit the newspapers. Everyone wants to see school bullying eradicated. No one seems to know how to do it.

What any particular school is doing about bullying depends on what administration and teachers know about the bullying dynamic, whether or not they feel bullying is necessarily a problem in their school, and the anti-bullying measures already in place. All of these elements are inherently affected by the many misconceptions that surround this issue.

Research into school bullying has assessed the effectiveness of what schools are currently doing and suggested ways to improve their approaches. Much of this research, unfortunately, remains known to relatively few. Without access to this research, teachers can easily fall prey to misconceptions about how best to tackle the issue. Bullying is a complex and emotional issue. This questionnaire is a simple test of how well-prepared you are to help guide your school's anti-bullying strategies.

See page 40 for answers to questionnaire.

Misconception or Research-Based Reality?

Read through the statements about bullying and decide which ones are misconceptions (M) and which ones represent practice based on how research reflects the reality of teaching (R).

1. Studies have shown that students in Grades 1 to 3 are not bullied as frequently as older students.   M or R?
2. A student can be either a bully or a target but not both.   M or R?
3. Teachers attend to between 10% and 20% of bullying situations.   M or R?
4. Adult bullying is a significant component of the school bullying problem.   M or R?
5. Student bullies are mostly boys.   M or R?
6. Using a peer-mediation model is an effective way to perform anti-bullying interventions.   M or R?
7. A majority of students hear homophobic slurs every day.   M or R?
8. Few teachers intervene in homophobic harassment situations.   M or R?
9. Gay-Straight Alliances usually include more straight than lesbian, gay, bisexual, or transgender members.   M or R?
10. Sexting among young people is a growing component of cyberbullying.   M or R?

The Bullying Dynamic

All schools, public and private, regardless of their location, student population, or academic success, have a problem with bullies. All students, regardless of their background, popularity, or academic or athletic success, can bully. Bullying can occur anywhere in a school and can be perpetrated by anyone in that school. In 2012, a national survey completed for the Public Health Agency of Canada found that 63% of children aged 11 to 15 said that bullies had targeted them. This study simply corroborates the alarming data from all over the world about bullying in schools.

International studies have found that anywhere from one-third to three-quarters of students have been involved in bullying situations. One study indicated that 160,000 students in the United States miss school each day due to bullying. Researchers from the University of Calgary reported in 2005 that half the students in their study had been bullied and that the students in Grades 1 to 3 were bullied as frequently as the students in Grades 4 to 6. Various studies have also found that 80% of bullying in schools is never reported (Parsons, 2005).

What constitutes bullying? The key component in any definition states that bullying is an abuse of the power imbalance that one person holds over another. That abuse can be physical, social, or emotional. Bullies often feel justified in their behavior and rely on bystanders or onlookers to do nothing about the bullying or to actually support their behavior.

The stereotypical image of an older, bigger student extorting lunch money from younger students is unfortunate and misleading. Bullying among students is far more diverse, pervasive, and insidious. Most bullying students deliberately use a variety of aggressive tactics to get what they want from someone else; they detect a pattern of aggression in the world around them and feel justified in their behavior. Punishment usually reinforces their sense that might is right.

Some student bullies see social interaction in terms of establishing and maintaining a hierarchy. They deliberately employ coercion, manipulation, and deception to solidify their dominance in the social pecking order and reinforce their sense of status and self-esteem. These students often present to adults as agreeable, well-meaning, confident, and capable individuals, yet reserve a totally different face for their targets. Their sense of entitlement, elitism, and arrogance absolves them of any kind of guilt.

Bullies are so egocentric and self-rationalizing that they usually feel provoked into their aggressive behavior and justify their actions by hinging them on insignificant or even invented slights. They understand social dynamics only in the context of competition and dominance. Since they have a reduced empathy for others, they have difficulty putting themselves in someone else's place. They feel powerful, superior, and self-confident enough to ignore the eventual dislike and isolation they sometimes engender among others.

Obviously, bullying in schools is a complicated and corrosive dynamic. Beyond the immediate harm done to those who are targeted, those who bully, those who are bullied, and those who stand witness to the bullying are all at risk for long-term negative consequences.

The one aspect of bullying in schools that no one talks about, however, and that accounts for the pivotal problem with combating bullying in schools is that bullies can be adults as well as students (Namie & Namie, 2003). An ongoing nationwide American survey consistently reports that the two worst professions for adults bullying other adults are nursing and teaching. And in schools, bullied teachers may feel justified in passing that bullying along to their students.

Color-coding Your School: The Bullying Culture

Bullied Teacher: Bullied Student (listed in the Bibliography on page 91) elaborates to a greater degree on themes and research found in this chapter.

What does all this mean for a school culture? Just suppose that overnight bullies magically turned red and their targets turned purple. When you enter your school the next day, what would you see? You would certainly notice the large number of students, anywhere from one-third to one-half of the school population, who bore the continuum of shades from pink to red and from mauve to purple. You would also realize that, while some students were entirely a shade of red and others entirely a shade of purple, a sizeable number were stained both red and purple.

As you continue your journey through the school, however, you're shocked to see that the principal who greets you with a big smile at the office door is a vivid fire-engine red and that the office administrator, head bowed to her computer, glows with an unsettling combination of red and purple.

As you stumble toward your own classroom, you're also disturbed at the number of red and purple colleagues and similarly colored parents dotting the hallways. You suddenly realize that the bullying dynamic is dauntingly complex: that individuals can be exclusively bullies, exclusively targets, or both bullies and targets; equally important, that bullies can be students or adults. When you reach the safety of your own classroom, you might well be afraid to look in the mirror.

Welcome to a bullying school culture.

Taken together, the students, teachers, principals, and parents constitute a school's bullying culture, with students occupying the lowest spot in the pecking order. Until all the elements in a school's bullying culture are addressed, the problem of student bullying can never be resolved. In most instances, schools treat bullying much like a case of flu that infects only students: apply a dose of medicine and it disappears. But bullying is more like a case of bubonic plague that infects everyone in the school's environment. Until the schoolwide contamination is rooted out and sterilized, a school's twin goals of nurturing and educating young people are continually undermined.

Bullying discourages risk-taking, and risk-taking lies at the heart of the learning/teaching process. When students feel free to take risks, they internally understand that mistakes and approximations are good. They feel free to experiment, to explore, or to try something new. In a bullying culture, on the other hand, students are constantly worrying if anything they present in public could be turned against them by the bullies around them. In a very direct sense, bullying poisons the learning/teaching environment in a school.

Teachers and students are vulnerable to bullying in schools for similar reasons. We expect a school to be a refuge from the outside world, a place where everyone is kept physically and emotionally safe and secure. Schools are responsible for inculcating the basic values of a society and, in fact, are supposed to mirror in microcosm how these values benefit both society and the individual.

In a school, everyone is expected to tell the truth, to follow the rules, to cooperate with one another for the good of all, and to accede to the decisions of authority figures. Highly aggressive individuals—whether adults or students—who lie, subvert the rules, compete unfairly for personal gain, or abuse the power they hold over others slowly and surely corrode the learning/teaching environment from the inside out. No one is safe.

Insights into Bullies and Targets

One of the many myths about bullying in schools contends that bullies target only the weak and, if targets would only develop backbones and stand up for themselves, bullying would disappear. Parents and teachers are both susceptible to this misguided line of thinking; but it's a case of "do as I say, not as I do." Adults certainly don't easily stand up to adult bullies. Psychologists Ruth and Gary Namie have pioneered studies of adult bullying in the workplace. They've discovered that 80% of adult bullies in the workplace are bosses, and that they commonly target the best and brightest of their employees.

Always keep in mind that bullying is an abuse of a power imbalance. Adults are well aware of how dangerous it can be to stand up to their bosses and speak truth to power. As a matter of fact, when adults stand up to a bullying boss, only about 20% of their co-workers will attempt to support them (Namie & Namie, 2003). The rest will side with the boss by remaining silent or will actually undermine their co-worker; they want to be on the winning side. In fact, it's so difficult for adult targets to defend themselves against workplace bullying that the Namies recommend that targets simply find another job if they can. When mature adults have this much trouble dealing with bullying, what chance do students have?

With students, targets for harassment are chosen for any number of reasons. Simply being a newcomer to a school without immediate friends or alliances might be enough to draw a bully's attention. A perceived slight, a manner of dress or deportment, association with a disliked peer or relative, or even success in school are reasons enough for one student to bully another. If bullies sense vulnerability in a target, they become emboldened and further empowered. They attempt to separate and isolate targets from their peer group by exploiting their targets' vulnerabilities.

Ethnocultural or religious minorities are always at risk of bullying. They can find themselves targeted for the color of their skin, their lack of English fluency, their lack of knowledge about sports or other recreational activities, the way they dress, what they eat, how they spend their free time, or what they believe.

Many students are constantly in a struggle to define and defend their place in the peer-group pecking order. Putdowns, slurs, jibes, and innuendo of all kinds are never purposeless or harmless; on the slippery slope of social acceptance, some students are struggling to maintain a toehold while others scheme to push the vulnerable to the bottom.

Bullies can further alienate their targets by forestalling a sympathetic backlash from the dominant student culture. Anyone in the peer group defending a vulnerable individual invites derision by association. Someone defending a target labelled "gay," for example, will themselves be labelled "gay." Even teachers are often reluctant to intervene in situations involving homophobic bullying for fear that a whisper campaign will be started about their own sexual orientation.

Bullying can be both convenient to overlook and difficult to uncover; teachers typically report that very little bullying goes on in their own school. Bullies are certainly careful to shield their behavior from adults and use threats and intimidation to silence their targets. When confronted, they claim they were "only kidding" or "fooling around." They might even accuse their targets of bullying them. Bystanders are ever ready to support a bully's lies—and not just from fear. Research has discovered that many bystanders often identify more closely with the bully's values; they seem to feel that targets deserve whatever they get.

The Code of Silence

Harassment in schools is endemic: even primary children are bullying as much as students in the later grades. Meanwhile, adults hypocritically advise students that telling about a bullying episode is the right course of action. Meanwhile, in the adult world, members of a peer group almost never "rat" or tell on another member. As a rule, police officers don't rat on other police officers, doctors don't rat on other doctors, lawyers don't rat on other lawyers, and politicians don't rat on other members of their political party.

During the G20 Conference in Toronto in 2010, for example, a number of police officers illegally covered their badge numbers; they wanted to act with impunity. Interestingly enough, if they couldn't be identified through video evidence, they were not held accountable for their actions, whatever they were. Eyewitness colleagues kept their mouths shut.

Although primary students tell on one another all the time, it isn't long before everyone learns how the world actually works. Even when offered protection

> If targets of bullying have physical, psychological, socio-economic, or sexual orientation differences as well, their vulnerability is compounded.

> Police officers who report the wrongdoing of other police officers can face ostracism and harassment. Sexual harassment in law enforcement is historically under-reported for this reason.

against retaliation, both targets and onlookers are reluctant to name the bullying behavior or name the bullies. Doing so always invites further and more widespread harassment, social ostracism, and ridicule. Students learn very quickly what the values are in the real world.

Not surprisingly, the adolescent code of silence is especially strong when boys bully girls. Boys expect and usually receive social sanction for "teasing," a form of relationship aggression that amounts to sexual harassment. They will throw their arms around a girl's neck at will, make sexually explicit comments or jokes, use sexual slurs like "slut" or "bitch," or spread unwarranted rumors. Girls are expected to endure this kind of hazing as a matter of course and are allowed to resist and respond only in a mild way, if at all.

In one survey, 80% of high-school girls reported they had been harassed (Parsons, 2005). If girls complain to a teacher about this kind of behavior, they risk scorn and retribution from both the boys and the other girls in their peer group. Onlookers will also assure the teacher that the boys "didn't mean anything" by their behavior and that the target was "too sensitive."

All schools have a bullying problem and all schools have a bullying culture. Within these cultures, students and adults mix and mingle in complicated and disturbing patterns, such as the following:

- Some students bully other students; some of these student bullies are themselves bullied by other student bullies; some of these student bullies bully teachers.
- Some teachers bully students; some teacher bullies bully other teachers; some teacher bullies bully parents and guardians.
- Some office staff bully teachers, students, and parents and guardians.
- Some principals bully teachers, office staff, students, and parents and guardians.
- Some parents bully teachers, office staff, principals, and their own and other people's children.

As these patterns illustrate, student bullying can't be resolved in isolation from the other components of a school's bullying culture. Anti-bullying programs will only succeed to the extent that the full nature, degree, and interrelationship of both student and adult bullying are addressed. By dealing directly and consistently with all aspects of bullying, teachers will discover that all the goals of the three laws of teaching are also addressed: students will feel safe, secure, and free to take risks in their learning; they will more readily engage with a stimulating classroom program and interact spontaneously with their peers; and, free from fear, will be able to enjoy how they learn as individuals.

Back to Square One

Anti-bullying Surveys

In the face of so much and so many different types of bullying, schools have difficulty finding effective solutions. Teachers typically attend to between 10% and 20% of bullying episodes (Parsons, 2005).

When you're losing a war, one way out is to declare victory and then disengage: that's the route most schools are taking in the war against school bullying. Board administrators encourage the view that bullying isn't a problem in their schools and principals are glad to oblige. Teachers are so overwhelmed, scaling their daily mountain of controlled chaos and front-line frustration, that they are more than willing to play along and turn a blind eye to an issue that seems ubiquitous and unmanageable.

But if the genuine will is there to rescue their learning/teaching environments, schools *can* effectively combat bullying. Research has established two components necessary for any anti- bullying initiative to succeed. The first is accountability.

See pages 41 and 44 for student assessment tools.

Before a school begins an anti-bullying program, the principal needs to implement several anonymous surveys to quantify, without naming names, the types of bullying specific to that school. Before creating an anti-bullying plan, a school must first discover what kind of bullying is going on, where, and how often. An anonymous survey will uncover if special-education students are being centred out for bullying, for example, or how much cyberbullying is going on, whether school monitors are abusing their positions, how widespread racial or homophobic harassment might be, or how often students are bullied going to and coming from school. A key here is to also give students an opportunity to comment on the nature and frequency of adult bullying they encounter. An anonymous student survey easily unearths the details specific to a school.

See page 49 for a survey for school staff.

Since an anti-bullying policy must apply to everyone in the school environment, especially the adult role models, all adults, including administrators, teachers, office staff, and janitorial and lunchroom assistants, must also complete an anonymous survey to discover the kind of adult bullying occurring in the school environment. Few schools or school boards have ever taken this step. If they don't, then any anti-bullying initiative is simply a sham. The principal acting disrespectfully to teachers in the hallways or classrooms, an office administrator who admonishes a tearful boy for "crying like a little girl," or teachers ignoring the cries of "ho," "fag," or "That's so gay!" are all aiding and abetting bullying. Adults telling racist, sexist, or homophobic jokes to one another in the office, staff room, or hallways are poisoning the environment even more.

Once the nature, frequency, and location of bullying in a school are discovered, anti-bullying initiatives based on that information can be devised and implemented.

For more extensive surveys that access information about bullies themselves and bystanders, see *Bullied Teacher: Bullied Student*, listed in the Bibliography on page 91.

A significant period of time (at least four or five months) after the initiative has been implemented and allowed to settle into routine, a second set of anonymous surveys will establish how effective the initiative has been. Up to now, board administrators have accepted their principals' anecdotal evidence that anti-bullying programs have indeed succeeded when, in fact, they have flared for a moment in a school's consciousness and then died away from lack of attention.

So the second crucial component of an anti-bullying strategy deals with how consistently the program is implemented throughout the school. Student bullies thrive on inconsistency. If they can point to a discrepancy in values from classroom to classroom, from principal to teacher, or from year to year, it fortifies their own sense that values are a relative commodity. No program will succeed on the basis of "do as I say, not as I do." The bullying culture in schools will remain impervious to anti-bullying programs until schools recognize that principals and their office staff also bully; so do teachers, and so do parents.

From the information gathered from these surveys, school staff can formulate a realistic anti-bullying program that focuses on the particular problems that an individual school might contain. Double standards, however, are destructive. For any anti-bullying initiative to be successful, all adults must interact with each other and with students in a fair, respectful, and equitable manner. At all times and throughout the school, school staff must insist on an environment completely free of sexist, racial, cultural, ability-related, and homophobic stereotyping. Bullying is a symptom, not a condition.

Day-to-day Tactics

How effectively the rules governing bullying in schools operate can be judged by the manner in which they are stated, the degree to which individuals accept their legitimacy, the consistency with which they are enforced, and the consequences for ignoring them.

Most schools by now have some sort of "no bullying" policy; however, the way the policy is phrased and posted can be problematic. We use the generic term "bullying" as a convenient way to refer to a wide range of verbal or written, physical, and social behaviors, such as physical or sexual assaults, relational exclusion, intimidation, and coercion. If you extend the definition to include antisocial behavior in cyberspace, the term becomes amorphous and its use with students counterproductive.

Oddly enough, when dealing with bullying episodes, it's best not to use any form of the word "bullying." In the first place, bullying takes on so many forms that students seldom self-identify as bullies. The popular star athlete who mercilessly hazes a physically inept peer, day after day, is simply "kidding around"; The Queen Bee (Wiseman, 2003) who has made it clear to her coterie that a peer is now to be shunned is merely exercising her right to choose her own friends; and the Internet-savvy student who impersonates a peer online and sets up a blog proclaiming the peer's gay life style feels entitled to behave any way he wants from the security of his own home computer. Complicating these attitudes is the rationalization that "everyone does it" and to be centred out for similar behavior is "unfair."

Students need to recognize the specific behaviors that constitute bullying before they can acknowledge their own involvement. Just as maximum speed limits are posted and recognized by drivers, the specific behaviors expected of all people in a school, students and adults alike, need to be clearly articulated, posted, and publicly acknowledged.

Interventions at school work best when the focus is removed from a particular target and placed in a neutral context. The goal is to assist all students to understand why such behavior occurs and how it affects everyone involved. Why does the aggressor feel justified in his or her behavior? What is prompting her or his actions? How are those actions affecting the target? What are the various ways in which bystanders react emotionally to the aggression? What motivates their behavior? As students work through the dynamic, they begin to realize that all three roles in this kind of bullying are linked.

Students also need the language to be able to talk about their actions and reactions. We want girls, for example, to be assertive, to make their feelings and needs known without hurting others. We want them to understand that at the core of aggressiveness is the desire to fulfil an individual's own needs at the expense of others. Awareness builds understanding: understanding breeds change.

Face-to-face encounters in a conflict-resolution format are effective only when both parties have similar influence and power. For that reason, never graft anti-bullying interventions onto a peer mediation model. You might not be aware that your well-liked, personable, and responsible peer mediator may well be a bully.

These sorts of encounters can be especially futile when dealing with relational bullying, which most often is exhibited between girls. Putting a relationship bully face-to-face with her target, especially in the presence of other girls in her clique, will often worsen the situation. The bully still possesses the power, and will use the opportunity to trivialize the behaviors, question the target's reactions, or blame the victim. At best, the bully will offer a perfunctory apology and continue the exclusion. The target, of course, will take the remedial episode as further proof that nothing can be done.

Targets of relational bullying need opportunities to meet with other students who have suffered similar kinds of exclusion. They need to understand that they aren't alone, they need opportunities to work through their feelings with sympathetic peers and an adult guide, and they need to develop strategies for dealing with their situations. In these groups they are able to reflect on, rehearse, and control their actions and reactions

Homophobic Bullying

People see gay and lesbian characters on TV, witness Pride parades around the world, observe the emergence of legalized same-sex marriage, and conclude that homophobia is a relic of the past and no longer an issue in schools. The research says otherwise. Just as homophobia remains embedded in our society, homophobia and homophobic bullying remain rooted and festering in our schools.

The cultural stigma of being gay, lesbian, or bisexual is so intense that bullies use homophobic slurs against anyone they want to dominate. An Egale Canada survey of 4000 teenagers, both homosexual and heterosexual, found that anti-gay comments are so common in Canadian schools that most students hear them on a daily basis: 70% of students said they heard phrases like "that's so gay" every day; almost 50% heard terms like "faggot," "lezbo," and "dyke" on a daily basis. (Egale, 2011)

Bullying of students who are actually gay, lesbian, or bisexual is of crisis proportions. According to a 2006 study in the *Journal of Adolescent Health*, 52% of gay or bisexual males attempted suicide, compared to 13 % of straight males. The Egale study discovered that two-thirds of lesbian, gay, and bisexual students said they felt unsafe at school, 51% had been verbally harassed about their sexual orientation, 21% had been physically or sexually harassed, and 45% had been sexually harassed at school. Against this poisonous onslaught, only 3% of teachers intervene in homophobic harassment, and then usually with a mild reprimand.

Empowering Gay-Straight Alliances

Of the various strategies for improving safety and well-being at school for LGBT (lesbian, gay, bisexual, transgender) students, gay-straight alliances (GSAs) have the greatest impact. Gay-straight alliances are student-led clubs for LGBT youth and their straight (heterosexual) peers with the goal of making the school community safe and amenable for all students. Regardless of sexual orientation, all students benefit from the opportunity to discuss, learn about, and understand the experiences and feelings associated with being LGBT in a predominantly straight school culture. Contrary to common perception, GSAs usually include more straight than LGBT students.

GLSEN (Gay, Lesbian and Straight Education Network) has been a leader in the struggle to end discrimination, harassment, and bullying based on sexual orientation, gender identity, and gender expression. The following guide for teachers and administrators who are considering the launch of a GSA in their school are based on GLSEN's suggestions:

- Inform the student body that school administration would be supportive of anyone wishing to start a GSA.
- Insist that anyone starting a GSA must first notify the school administration and also be prepared to follow the rules and procedures for establishing any school club.
- Require the GSA to have a faculty advisor to act as liaison to administration and mentor for the group. The group should seek out its own choice for faculty advisor from among various sympathetic staff members. The staff member can be of any sexual orientation.
- Make sure that school guidance counsellors and social workers are prepared to act as resource personnel for the group. They may be able to speak to students who might be interested in joining the club and offer the club suggestions for outreach programs, such as days of awareness, speakers for assemblies, or teacher in-service.
- Provide a safe, secure, and private meeting place within the school; a small food budget to allow the participants to mingle over snacks would increase the casual and welcoming nature of the meetings.
- Encourage the group to put up LGBT-positive posters to let all students know that the school is cultivating a positive dialogue about the associated issues; be prepared for possible conflict, such as the posters being vandalized and torn down, but encourage the group to continue putting up new ones until the violence dissipates. The posters should include what a GSA is and what it does, how to make contact if interested in attending a meeting, and the fact that anyone and everyone will be welcomed.
- Direct the LGBT group to resources, such as GLSEN's website, that will help them with practical suggestions for holding their meetings; confidentiality and open-ended discussions are key components.
- Request that the group set up an action plan for the future with creative ideas for making the school a more equitable and bully-free culture.

Teachers and administration need to be ready to support the group in any way they can. The fact that the school needs a GSA is a clear indication that homophobic bullying is a serious issue in the school. The more vocal and forceful the opposition to such a club becomes, the more obvious it is that the school has deep-lying problems with homophobic bullying. Finally, the school must accept that the successful launching of a GSA will alleviate but not resolve the issue of homophobic bullying. A GSA is a first step, not a total solution.

Research supporting the benefits of GSAs and a wealth of resources can be found at www.glsen.org and MyGSA.ca, the first Canadian website on GSAs in schools.

The Cyberbullying Epidemic

One of the downsides of the computer age has been the natural fit between the computer and relationship aggression. The first law of teaching requires teachers to understand and confront this new threat to their students' well-being before they even consider powering up their school's computers: teachers must keep their students physically and emotionally safe, and feeling good about themselves and what they're doing.

Cyberbullying is the purposeful attempt to harm someone else through the use of information and communication technologies. Cyberbullying encompasses relationship aggression and all manner of electronic threatening, and it's ubiquitous. Hurtful text or images are posted via e-mail, cell phone, Twitter, instant messaging, blogs, and chat rooms. Cyberbullying can assume a variety of forms, such as harassment, denigration, impersonation, exclusion, outing (posting a secret or embarrassing information or image), threatening, or stalking.

As use of the Internet has exploded among young people, so has cyberbullying. As vulnerable students turn more and more to social networking, they are placing themselves in constant jeopardy. Teachers and parents have been slow to recognize how early in life students latch on to the habit and how all-consuming it can be.

A 2010 survey by the Kaiser Family Foundation found that the average 8- to 18-year-old spends approximately 7.5 hours a day online. A June 2011 study by Consumer Reports found that Facebook had 7.5 million users under age 13, including 5 million aged 10 or younger. Few, if any, students that age have the maturity and experience necessary to manipulate and navigate through such a sophisticated social medium.

The relative impersonal nature of e-mail, Twitter, instant messaging, and chat rooms frees aggressors from normal restraints and puts targets in added jeopardy. Bullies can easily post offensive messages and photographs; with a few keystrokes those messages can appear anywhere.

Along with the usual reasons for not reporting bullying, students are also afraid that reporting this kind of bullying will lead to their social networking being curtailed or more closely supervised by an adult. Being disconnected from the virtual reality of cyberspace seems to be a fate worse than the bullying they endure. Finally, just as in real life, targets may feel that if the bully is silenced, the friends of the bully might retaliate en masse.

What complicates the issue even further is that many students hold the mistaken belief that there are no rules on the Internet; therefore, bullies are allowed to say anything they want. In the same vein, students might have been targeted while engaging in risky or unwise behavior online, behavior they rationalize as permitted in the unregulated environment of the Internet but still punishable by their parents. Adults, for example, are astonished at the amount of sexting occurring among young people.

Sexting is sending sexual photos, video, or text from one cell phone to another. A 2009 telephone poll by the Pew Research Center's Internet and American Life Project discovered that 5% of 14- to 17-year-olds had sent naked or nearly naked photos or videos to someone else. An Internet poll for the Associated Press and MTV found that 24% of 14- to 17-year-olds had been involved in sexting. Given the reticence of young people to admit what goes on in their culture, the practice of sexting could be even more widespread.

While individuals may feel secure in sexting to a girlfriend or boyfriend, once the relationship sours, the images and messages find new and wider exposure throughout the electronic media. While boys and girls appear to indulge in the practice equally, girls are more liable to suffer social scorn and ostracism when their images and words are publicized. Once they've been ridiculed as a "slut" or "ho" by their peer group, these unfortunate young women have little recourse.

Answers to the questionnaire on page 30:

1. M
2. M
3. R
4. R
5. M
6. M
7. R
8. R
9. R
10. R

Even if they locate to another school, their images remain embedded in the virtual reality of cyberspace and can follow them anywhere.

Bullying always includes the abuse of a power imbalance; with cyberbullying, however, that concept is more ambiguous. Certainly, bullies in the real world may continue their antisocial behavior online; however, someone who feels powerless or is targeted in the real world might attempt to turn the tables online and try to empower themselves through online aggression.

Mass messaging, cyberstalking, or negative postings about someone on a personal website can be emotionally devastating. And there's no escape from the abuse. Whatever happens online is carried into the schoolyard, the classroom, and the school computer room. With the proliferation of smart phones adding to online access, bullying can now go on 24 hours a day.

Going Offline: Dealing with Cyberbullying

To be effective in routing out and eradicating this kind of bullying, teachers must be prepared to examine and intervene in the personal lives of their students, and to pursue signs of misbehavior within and without the classroom walls. The day has long passed when it was possible to believe that school ends at the school's front door.

The first line of defence against cyberbullying is the school's anti-bullying policy. The policy must make clear that bullying will not be tolerated in any form, including electronic. Specific violations should be detailed and consequences listed. The policy should also articulate that it's a criminal offence to repeatedly communicate with someone in a way that causes them fear for their safety or for the safety of others. Students need to agree in writing to abide by the terms and conditions that describe the appropriate use of electronic media; parents need to sign as well, to indicate that they have read the policy and agree to the terms and conditions. Failure to sign on the part of the student and/or the parent or guardian would result in the student's electronic participation being constantly monitored and severely curtailed.

Next comes the hard part. Parents and teachers have to work as a team to supervise students' online behavior at home and at school; they have to act decisively when warranted. An information meeting should be held at the school to give parents and teachers the most up-to-date facts about online and Internet behavior. A summary of what experts have to say on the issue should form part of a school newsletter. Parents should be encouraged to contact the school whenever they have questions or concerns, and the school must immediately contact the home when a student breaches the policy. Parents need to check e-mail accounts at home to find out who is on their child's personal network. They also need to check their child's phone for the nicknames and codes that might supply clues to online screen names. Stopping the behavior at school merely stops the behavior at school. Unless parents are involved, cyberbullies are free to trot home and turn on the power.

Bullying and My School: A Junior Student Survey

Names are not needed.

We want to stop all bullying in this school. We need your help to find out what kind of bullying is going on this year. You **don't** need to put your name of this survey. We **don't** want you to name other people.

What is bullying?

Bullying means to hurt someone in some way. Bullying can be done by one person or more than one person. Bullying also means that the same person or persons do the hurting more than once. Some bullies hurt other people by doing physical things like hitting, kicking, or throwing things. Some bullies threaten to do things to you unless you give them money or obey them. Some bullies make you feel bad by name-calling, telling lies about you, or trying to get people not to be your friend.

Information About You

❑ I am a girl   ❑ I am a boy

I am in Grade _____

How You Have Been Bullied

This section asks about how you have been bullied. Please remember that it has to be the same person or persons doing this to you more than once. Please circle the number in each statement that best fits what happened to you this year in school. Here is what the numbers mean:

1 = never   2 = sometimes   3 = about once a week   4 = more than once a week

This year in school someone bullied me by…

doing things like hitting, punching, or throwing things.

1   2   3   4

hurting me with a weapon like a stick, ruler, knife, or something else.

1   2   3   4

threatening to hurt me.

1   2   3   4

saying things about my body or saying sexual things that made me feel uncomfortable, embarrassed, or afraid.

1   2   3   4

touching my body or my clothes in an inappropriate way.

1   2   3   4

making me give them money or other things.

1   2   3   4

1 = never   2 = sometimes   3 = about once a week   4 = more than once a week

making me do what they told me to when I didn't want to.

1   2   3   4

saying hurtful things about my skin color, the country I came from, or my religion.

1   2   3   4

calling me terrible, hurtful names.

1   2   3   4

spreading untrue stories or gossip about me.

1   2   3   4

trying to make others not be my friend and leave me out of things.

1   2   3   4

passing around a hurtful, untrue note about me.

1   2   3   4

sending me a hurtful, untrue e-mail or text message.

1   2   3   4

posting a hurtful, untrue message about me on an Internet site.

1   2   3   4

This is another way I was bullied that isn't on this survey.

This year, I have been bullied in some way this often:

1   2   3   4

Pembroke Publishers ©2012 *Back to Learning* by Les Parsons ISBN 978-1-55138-281-4

Where You Have Been Bullied

This section asks **where** in the school you have been bullied or **where** you have watched someone else being bullied. Your name is not on this paper. Please answer honestly. Circle the number in each statement that best fits what happened to you this year in school. Here is what the numbers mean:

1 = never   2 = sometimes   3 = about once a week   4 = more than once a week

This year in school I was bullied or watched someone else being bullied…

in the schoolyard.

1   2   3   4

in the school hallways.

1   2   3   4

in a classroom.

1   2   3   4

in the gym.

1   2   3   4

in the washroom.

1   2   3   4

in the lunchroom.

1   2   3   4

on the way to school.

1   2   3   4

on the way home from school.

1   2   3   4

on the school bus.

1   2   3   4

in this place in or around the school not mentioned in the survey:

This is the end of the survey. Thank you for helping us get rid of bullying in this school.

Pembroke Publishers ©2012 *Back to Learning* by Les Parsons ISBN 978-1-55138-281-4

Bullying and My School: An Intermediate Student Survey

Names are not needed.

We want to stop all bullying in this school. We need your help to find out what kind of bullying is going on this year. This survey is meant to be anonymous. We **don't** want you to put your name on this survey. We **don't** want you to name other people.

What is bullying?

Bullying means to hurt someone physically, emotionally, or socially by using some kind of power one person or more has over another person. Although one incident of bullying can be devastating, most definitions of bullying require that the same person or persons bully more than once. The survey includes specific examples of different kinds of bullying, including a section on electronic bullying.

Information About You

❑ I am a girl   ❑ I am a boy

I am in Grade _____

How You Have Been Bullied

This section asks about how you have been bullied. Please remember that it has to be the same person or persons doing this to you more than once. Please circle the number in each statement that best fits what happened to you this year in school. Here is what the numbers mean:

1 = never   2 = sometimes   3 = about once a week   4 = more than once a week

This year in school someone bullied me by…

hurting me in a physical way, such as by tripping, hitting, punching, or throwing things.

1   2   3   4

threatening to hurt me in a physical way, such as by tripping, hitting, punching, or throwing things.

1   2   3   4

hurting me with a weapon like a pair of scissors, a knife, or something else.

1   2   3   4

threatening to hurt me with a weapon like a pair of scissors, a knife, or something else.

1   2   3   4

saying things about my body image that made me feel uncomfortable, embarrassed, or ashamed.

1   2   3   4

saying sexual things that made me feel uncomfortable, embarrassed, or afraid.

1   2   3   4

Pembroke Publishers ©2012 *Back to Learning* by Les Parsons ISBN 978-1-55138-281-4

1 = never   2 = sometimes   3 = about once a week   4 = more than once a week

taunting me with name-calling, such as "gay," "dyke," or other kinds of terrible, hurtful names.

1   2   3   4

touching my body or my clothes in an inappropriate way.

1   2   3   4

forcing me to give them money or other things.

1   2   3   4

forcing me to do what they told me to when I didn't want to.

1   2   3   4

saying hurtful things about my cultural or racial background.

1   2   3   4

saying hurtful things about my religion.

1   2   3   4

saying hurtful things about my gender.

1   2   3   4

saying hurtful things about my disability.

1   2   3   4

saying hurtful things about my sexual orientation.

1   2   3   4

saying hurtful things about my poor grades or marks.

1   2   3   4

saying hurtful things about my excellent grades or marks.

1   2   3   4

spreading untrue stories or gossip about me.

1   2   3   4

trying to make others not be my friend and leave me out of things.

1   2   3   4

passing around a hurtful untrue note about me.

1   2   3   4

1 = never   2 = sometimes   3 = about once a week   4 = more than once a week

This year the person who bullied me…

was someone the teachers liked and admired.

1   2   3   4

was under the influence of alcohol.

1   2   3   4

was under the influence of drugs.

1   2   3   4

Cyberbullying

This next section asks about **cyberbullying**. Cyberbullying refers to all kinds of electronic aggression and threatening. Hurtful text or images are posted via such means as e-mail, cell phone, Twitter, instant messaging, blogs, or chat rooms.

Cyberbullying can assume a variety of forms, such as harassing, bad-mouthing, impersonating someone, excluding, outing (posting a secret or embarrassing information or image), threatening, or stalking. Please circle the number in each statement that best fits what happened to you this year in school. Here is what the numbers mean:

1 = never   2 = sometimes   3 = about once a week   4 = more than once a week

This year someone bullied me electronically…

during school hours.

1   2   3   4

before or after school hours.

1   2   3   4

This year someone bullied me electronically by…

sending me a hurtful, untrue e-mail or text message.

1   2   3   4

posting a hurtful, untrue message about me on a social networking site, blog, or chat room.

1   2   3   4

posting some secret or embarrassing information or image.

1   2   3   4

pretending to be me and saying terrible untrue things I would never say.

1   2   3   4

Pembroke Publishers ©2012 *Back to Learning* by Les Parsons ISBN 978-1-55138-281-4

1 = never   2 = sometimes   3 = about once a week   4 = more than once a week

threatening me.

1   2   3   4

sending me text messages or images of a sexual nature.

1   2   3   4

harassing or stalking me.

1   2   3   4

This is another way I was bullied that wasn't on this survey.

This year I have been bullied in some way this often:

1   2   3   4

Where You Have Been Bullied

This section asks where in the school you have been bullied or where you have watched someone else being bullied. Your name is not on this paper. Please answer honestly. Circle the number in each statement that best fits what happened to you this year in school. Here is what the numbers mean:

1 = never   2 = sometimes   3 = about once a week   4 = more than once a week

This year in school I was bullied or watched someone else being bullied…

in the schoolyard or anywhere else outside on school property.

1   2   3   4

in the school hallways.

1   2   3   4

in a classroom.

1   2   3   4

in the library.

1   2   3   4

in the computer lab.

1   2   3   4

Pembroke Publishers ©2012 *Back to Learning* by Les Parsons ISBN 978-1-55138-281-4

1 = never   2 = sometimes   3 = about once a week   4 = more than once a week

in the gym.

1   2   3   4

in the change rooms

1   2   3   4

in the washroom.

1   2   3   4

in the cafeteria or lunchroom.

1   2   3   4

on the way to school.

1   2   3   4

on the way home from school.

1   2   3   4

on the school bus.

1   2   3   4

on the street or in my neighborhood

1   2   3   4

in this place in or around the school not mentioned in the survey:

This is the end of the survey. Thank you for helping us get rid of bullying in this school.

Bullying and My School: Tool for Adult School Assessment and Reflection

In this reflection survey, please indicate the extent to which you agree or disagree that each statement correctly describes the dominant behavior in your school.

A. Determining the School Tone

1 = strongly disagree   2 = disagree   3 = agree   4 = strongly agree

Staff displays a respectful attitude toward all students.

1   2   3   4

Students display a respectful attitude toward all adults.

1   2   3   4

Students display a respectful attitude toward one another.

1   2   3   4

Administrators seldom display bullying behavior.

1   2   3   4

Teachers seldom display bullying behavior.

1   2   3   4

Support staff (secretaries, custodians, etc.) seldom display bullying behavior.

1   2   3   4

Parents/guardians seldom display bullying behavior when in the school or on the school grounds.

1   2   3   4

Visiting board personnel (superintendents, trustees, consultants) seldom display bullying behavior.

1   2   3   4

Students seldom display bullying behavior.

1   2   3   4

B. Identifying School Anti-bullying Policies

1 = strongly disagree   2 = disagree   3 = agree   4 = strongly agree

The school has a written policy regarding bullying.

1   2   3   4

A copy of the school's anti-bullying policy has been sent home this year to parents/guardians.

1   2   3   4

A parent/guardian information night regarding the school's anti-bullying policy has been or will be held this school year.

1   2   3   4

A school assembly regarding the school's anti-bullying policy has been or will be held this school year.

1   2   3   4

Teachers have been directed to review the school's anti-bullying policy with their students this term.

1   2   3   4

The school's anti-bullying policy clearly states specific sanctions and the specific behaviors that trigger these sanctions.

1   2   3   4

The school's anti-bullying approach contains options for some form of anger management, impulse control, and the development of empathy in bullies.

1   2   3   4

The school's anti-bullying approach includes some form of adult-led talk-therapy support for targets.

1   2   3   4

The school has a written code of behavior regarding electronic communications (computers, texting, cell phones, etc.) that includes dealing with forms of electronic bullying.

1   2   3   4

The written code of behavior regarding electronic bullying has been sent home this year to parents/guardians.

1   2   3   4

Students comply with the policy on electronic bullying.

1   2   3   4

C. Implementing the Anti-bullying Policies

1 = strongly disagree   2 = disagree   3 = agree   4 = strongly agree

A staff meeting has been held this year to discuss bullying and anti-bullying measures.

1   2   3   4

Teaching staff have been in-serviced within the past two years on the nature of bullying and what to do about it.

1   2   3   4

Pembroke Publishers ©2012 *Back to Learning* by Les Parsons ISBN 978-1-55138-281-4

Teaching staff have been in-serviced within the past two years on the nature of adult bullying and what to do about it.

1   2   3   4

Administrators agree with all aspects of the anti-bullying policy.

1   2   3   4

Administrators consistently impose sanctions for bullying whenever they are warranted.

1   2   3   4

Administrators correctly use intervention strategies instead of, or as well as, sanctions when warranted.

1   2   3   4

Teachers agree with all aspects of the anti-bullying policy.

1   2   3   4

Bullying behavior among students is never tolerated in the classroom.

1   2   3   4

Administrators never tolerate bullying behavior by and among adults.

1   2   3   4

Teachers are on time for their supervisory duties.

1   2   3   4

Teachers accept responsibility for supervising students anywhere in the building or on school grounds.

1   2   3   4

Bullying behavior among students is never tolerated anywhere in the school building or on school grounds.

1   2   3   4

Staff strictly enforce the code of behavior regarding electronic bullying.

1   2   3   4

Administration strictly enforces the code of behavior regarding electronic bullying.

1   2   3   4

D. Evaluating the State of Bullying in the School

1 = strongly disagree   2 = disagree   3 = agree   4 = strongly agree

The teaching staff was surveyed at some time this year to ascertain the extent and nature of bullying in the school.

1   2   3   4

The non-teaching staff was surveyed at some time this year to ascertain the extent and nature of bullying in the school.

1   2   3   4

The students were surveyed at some time this year to ascertain the extent and nature of bullying in the school.

1   2   3   4

The parents/guardians were surveyed at some time this year to ascertain the extent and nature of bullying in the school.

1   2   3   4

The school has some mechanism for determining each year the success of anti-bullying measures.

1   2   3   4

A safe, orderly, and equitable environment is maintained throughout the school.

1   2   3   4

E. Identifying the Degree of Collaboration Within the School

1 = strongly disagree   2 = disagree   3 = agree   4 = strongly agree

Administration uses cooperative learning strategies with teachers.

1   2   3   4

Teachers use cooperative learning strategies with students.

1   2   3   4

Administration and staff work together as a mutually supportive team.

1   2   3   4

Teachers have meaningful input into setting the agenda for staff meetings.

1   2   3   4

Teachers have meaningful input into budget, timetable, and curricular priorities.

1   2   3   4

3

Literacy in the Digital Universe

The interface between the digital universe and education is a shifting, uneasy area; curriculum in today's world seems to be overwhelmed by the capabilities of computers and the potential of the Internet. Teachers often see themselves as merely facilitators for the next technological innovation. Technology leads: teachers follow.

See page 65 for answers to questionnaire.

Misconception or Research-Based Reality?

Read through the following statements about literacy and technology, and decide which ones are misconceptions (M) and which ones represent practice based on how research reflects the reality of teaching (R).

1. Blogging among young people is increasing.   M or R?
2. A number of employees of Silicon Valley companies, such as Google, Apple, and Yahoo, send their children to a school without computers. M or R?
3. Most business leaders say that, among high-school graduates, written skills—such as memos, letters, or technical reports—and critical thinking skills are especially deficient.   M or R?
4. People who multitask among iPods, e-mails, texting, Twitter, and cell phones are quicker at task switching than those who don't.   M or R?
5. Cell phones and other mobile devices outnumber human beings in the United States.   M or R?
6. Most children age two or younger do not have an online presence. M or R?
7. When we make quick decisions based on limited information, these decisions are usually right.   M or R?
8. Wall Street traders employ powerful computers to speed-read articles, blog posts, and Tweets to interpret the words and then to trade on them.   M or R?
9. In school reading programs, asking questions does little to foster thinking and question answering provides little good evidence of understanding.   M or R?
10. Affective and cognitive behaviors are two sides of the same coin. M or R?

The digital universe remains a text-based world. Today, as in the past, teaching literacy is one of a teacher's major responsibilities. But teachers are grappling with how to approach that task with today's computer-savvy students. How much reading instruction, for example, should be left to computer programs? How do you teach literacy to students with a "point and click" mentality without boring them? What does literacy even mean in the computer age? The questionnaire on page 53 can help set the stage for a discussion of these issues.

As teachers struggle to define their role in the electronic age, the three laws of teaching can transform how they look at and operate within the digital universe.

The Electronic Illusion

Whatever their personal feelings about the impact of digital technology, teachers have a vital role to play in how it evolves. As the first law of teaching directs, tackling the issue of cyberbullying is a teacher's first priority (see Chapter 2, page 38). The next challenge for teachers is to provide the skills necessary for students to reflect thoughtfully on how to process the deluge of vicarious experience from the digital universe and become aware of how and why they are extracting meaning in the specific way they do.

Teachers are fond of saying that their students know more about computers than they do. But they mistake a familiarity and facility with the superficial aspects of manipulating electronic devices for a mature and thoughtful appreciation of an inert and seemingly limitless store of information. Teachers see students constantly texting back and forth, downloading music and DVDs, accessing Facebook and YouTube, or setting up personal blogs, and infer students are capable of mature, articulate interaction.

But are students sharing terse, reflective thoughts or banal observations and trite social interactions? From 2006 to 2009, for example, blogging among young people aged 12 to 17 fell by half. They prefer updates in Facebook and Twitter to writing longer entries (Patil, 2011). Author Neal Gabler fears that the Internet age is drowning us in data at the expense of thinking. He believes "we live in a post-Enlightenment age in which rationality, science, logical argument and debate have lost the battle in many sectors to superstition, faith, opinion, and orthodoxy." In this age, people value knowing over thinking because ideas have less immediate value than data that can be immediately monetized. In a situation that mirrors bad money driving out good (Gresham's Law), "trivial information pushes out significant information" and "information, trivial or not, pushes out ideas." (Gabler, 2011)

Three-quarters of business leaders, meanwhile, report that even when students complete high school, their applied skills, such as work ethic, accountability, punctuality, working with others, and time and workload management, are deficient. A greater number say that written skills, such as memos, letters, or technical reports, and critical thinking skills are especially deficient (Corporate Voices for Working Families, 2008).

Even computer-savvy technocrats are having second thoughts about the impact of computers on education. A number of employees of Silicon Valley companies, such as Google, Apple, and Yahoo, send their children to a school without computers (*New York Times*, 2011). At the Waldorf School of the Peninsula, the focus is on creative activity-based learning. These parents believe that, if their children are exposed to computers too early, their creative thinking, movement, human

The Three Laws of Teaching

1. Teachers must keep their students physically and emotionally safe.
2. Teachers must offer their students interesting and stimulating learning activities.
3. Teachers must keep their students feeling good about how they're learning.

interaction, and attention spans will be negatively affected. They certainly don't believe that their children need computers to find interesting and stimulating things to do. At the same time, they believe that contemporary technology has made computers so user-friendly that their children can easily pick up the skills they require at a later date.

They have some grounds for their concerns. A recent Stanford University study, for example, discovered that people who multitask among iPods, e-mails, texting, Twitter, and cell phones are less capable than those who don't in three significant areas: they are slower at task switching, they are unable to ignore irrelevant information, and they have more difficulty keeping organized the information that their brains gather (*New York Times*, 2011).

We need to be cautious, then, about the capabilities with which we invest our students. When we witness them constantly jumping into the Internet, we assume they fully understand how to manage the taps of this reservoir of information when, in fact, they're just as likely to drown in a sea of indecipherable data. Just as being a whiz at Monopoly doesn't qualify you to be a stockbroker, the skills and values developed through playing the various versions of the militaristic Call of Duty won't prepare students for researching on the Web.

The Electronic Pied Piper

Many students these days are far more comfortable in cyberspace than they are in the classroom. Electronic media, in fact, are students' primary sources for news, knowledge, recreational activities, and, increasingly, personal interactions. At home, on the street, on the subway, or in the school hallways, they are plugged into their smartphones, tablets, laptops, or mp3 players. Specially designed video productions deliver stories to the web and mobile devices in short bursts, paid for through product placements. The newer phones even contain gaming capabilities.

Cell phones and other mobile devices, in fact, outnumber human beings in the United States. With voice recognition and control capabilities, the new generation of devices have even done away with the need for keypads. One voice command and students are locked onto the Internet to check the bus schedule, catch up on the latest Tweets, or find out where everyone is meeting for lunch.

Who knows where the digital Pied Piper will lead? Chaos theory predicts that, in a system of circular feedback, a small change in initial conditions can cause huge and unpredictable changes as the future unfolds. The social network Facebook is a case in point. Initially conceived by frat boys as a way to meet girls, it quickly and unexpectedly evolved to play a crucial role in promoting societal revolutions. And everyone is climbing on board. *Harper's* Magazine revealed that, as of December 2011, 92% of children age two or younger had an online presence.

Each day, students constantly surf a relentless flood of language, images, concepts, and values that trigger emotions and shape their understanding of reality. They're also attracted to and a target for the rumors, distortions, and fabrications embedded in the unending stream of data. As spam continues to latch on to and infect every communication device invented with unwanted commercial messages, the old-time siren calls of sex and sensationalism compete for the reflexive clicks that are the yardstick of success for Internet entrepreneurs.

As students interact with this torrent of data and with each other in increasingly novel and ingenious ways, using increasingly more sophisticated and user-friendly technology, predictions about the future abound. Some seers see the digital age as a simple movement back to the future: the Internet is no more than a bigger and better library. Others see humans developing new and better ways of thinking as information and decision-making become increasingly democratized. And others predict a dimming of intelligence and a lemming-like stampede to revere the superficial.

Technology or Teaching

With the ever-expanding technology battering the educational systems like a tsunami and reconfiguring the shape of an unknown future, what role are teachers expected to play? Digital technology, social networking, and the ubiquitous Internet leave many teachers feeling like polar bears on rapidly melting ice floes. Change is occurring so rapidly that teachers' very existence is threatened by the disappearance of their school's traditional parameters. And their students are more than willing to tell them how out of the loop they are.

Like deer frozen in the headlights, teachers watch dumfounded as their students Twitter and Tweet in a brave new electronic age. Shell-shocked by progress too radical and swift to be comprehended, they remain on the sidelines, mystified, paralyzed, demoralized, and irrelevant, while their students effortlessly outstrip them.

Many teachers would agree with the sentiments expressed at a meeting of the Ontario Education Association attended by 10,000 beleaguered educators: "How can we deal with a knowledge explosion that leaves our lessons outdated as we teach them? How can we cover everything modern society expects us to teach?"

Of course, that meeting was held in 1965.

In his book, *Crawling from the Wreckage*, Gwynne Dyer offers a refreshing rebuttal to the common argument that computers have created change too rapid to comprehend. He asks us to consider how we would cope if, over the course of 50 years, we had to adjust to railways, steamships, and the telegraph; the proliferation of huge urban settlements and the resultant social movement; and the impact of Darwinism and Marxism.

That's what happened between 1825 and 1875.

Consider, as well, if, over the course of 50 years, we had to adjust to gaslight being replaced by electricity and horses being replaced by cars; if we were inundated in the same period by the growing presence of radio, telephones, and refrigerators, new forms of education and entertainment, and the soul-destroying impact of mass warfare on a level never before seen.

That's what happened between 1875 and 1925.

Compared to Dyer's examples, the "information technological revolution" has been a ubiquitous, if underwhelming, presence. Digital technology has given us more rapid communication and calculation power, access to a vast library of data that ranges from the profound to the lunatic, 24/7 social interaction, non-stop commercialization of digital media, and endless waves of vapidly diverting minutiae and pornography.

School boards, on the other hand, seem to think that in the electronic age students can practically teach themselves. They point to the technological advances that prove that their schools are on the cutting edge of the educational revolution: the number of computers in their schools; the number of students from Kindergarten on up that regularly use them; the wireless connections that facilitate access to the Internet; the digital textbooks and dictionaries that the schools now utilize to cut costs, and the amount of research being done on the Web.

Although it sounds like science fiction, schools themselves are moving into cyberspace. In this brave new world, a school no longer has to be held in a building and students never need to physically meet face to face. Traditional schools are turning into space-age cyberschools. As of December 2011, 250,000 students in the United States were enrolled full-time in cyberschools (*Harper's*, October 2011).

In education, moreover, the current rallying cry is, "The book is dead: long live the e-book!" School boards are falling all over themselves in the rush to invest in wireless e-readers and digital textbooks. High-school students will soon possess e-readers that have their textbooks, support materials, and yearly organizers enclosed. Along with the current embedded dictionaries, the goal is to eventually add audio and video functions to produce a fully interactive electronic learning/teaching experience.

But dig a little deeper and you find the educational love affair with computers is more flash than substance. Take the issue of computer research.

It's easy to see why students love to do research on the Web: point, click, copy a few times, and the project is finished—and it looks great! If they have an old-fashioned teacher, they package the wealth of information, the pictures and graphs, and the purloined references in a duotang, add a customized photoshopped title page, and an *A* can't be far behind. Those with more computer-literate teachers simply upload the material to their school file and wait for their *A* to be clicked back to them.

Since many students believe there are no rules on the Internet, they can't understand what's wrong with using what other people have put out there free of charge. Besides, downloading is a way of life: viral videos, celebrity news, pictures, games, music, and DVDs are whizzing around through cyberspace all the time. The Internet is regarded as an inexhaustible "replicator" on a virtual starship; anything you need can be copied and utilized. The Internet cornucopia just keeps on giving.

But the Internet is inert: it's not a giant brain and it doesn't think. What it does resemble is an interlocking series of multilane roadways, overpasses, and tunnels with images and words shooting every which way and few road signs, speed restrictions, maps, or regulations to guide and protect the unwary traveler. For these reasons, students need a comprehensive series of driving lessons and tests before they're ready to effectively access the information on the Internet highways. They have to acquire and be able to apply a sophisticated set of interrelated skills to effectively navigate a host of pitfalls they'll meet along the way.

Parsing the New Literacy

Regardless of whether students are accessing a website or opening a text message, reading an e-book or a paperback, trying to form an opinion from a blog entry or a newspaper editorial, the skills required to make sense of their environment remain the same as before the computer was ever invented. Literacy in the digital age, in fact, is more important than it ever was. After joining the battle against cyberbullying, a teacher's next task is based on the second law of teaching: the teacher needs to offer students interesting and stimulating learning activities to increase their literacy skills. First, however, teachers need to understand the complexities of that task.

Through the Internet and e-books, students have access to more print material and more difficult-to-understand print material than they've ever had. They also have to discriminate among countless articles and books to determine which ones are relevant to their search needs and abilities to comprehend, and the relevant objectivity and validity of the content. The overwhelming amount of material, the difficulties separating fact from opinion, and the mature skills required to sift through it all quickly and efficiently are daunting enough for an adult, let alone a Grade 5 student. No wonder plagiarism is high on every school's alert list.

The technology of the electronic age is misleading: the superficial multitasking that students quickly master can actually mask their inadequate literacy and numeracy skills and their unfamiliarity with critical thinking. Given the increasingly user-friendly aspect of technology, students understandably opt for the easy-to-do at the expense of the difficult-to-learn. The swiftness and immediacy of electronic media can even promote and enshrine a system for organizing knowledge that leads to poor decision-making.

In his book, *Thinking, Fast and Slow*, Daniel Kahneman describes two kinds of interrelated thinking that he calls System One and System Two. System One makes quick decisions based on limited information. Whether it's recognizing a face or making a split-second Tweet, System One is able to access our memory base of strong emotions, especially fear, pain, and hatred, as it makes immediate decisions. These decisions are often wrong.

In System Two, the brain forms judgments more slowly and deliberately in a process of conscious thinking and critical appraisal of data. System Two evaluates the decisions made by System One and revises them as needed. System Two is more reliable, far-reaching, and insightful: but it's also hard work. In time and calories, System Two thinking is costly and we tend to avoid this kind of mental expenditure whenever possible. Kahneman believes that the day-to-day routine tasks of informal talking, writing without reflection, and calculating are substitutes for deep and deliberate thinking.

See page 10 for a discussion of how students have learned to equate effort with failure.

The danger for students embedded in the electronic culture is the easy immediacy of their interactions; in other words, their reliance on System One thinking. Electronic gaming, social networking, or Internet surfing are all based on instant response and gratification. To *work* at thinking is not only an unfamiliar approach to problem-solving but also, in this narcissistic culture, an admission of failure. Far better to post your problem on Facebook, survey the response of your "friends," and let the majority solve your problem for you.

With two thumbs poised over a tiny keypad, students have even found a way to force written language to conform to their communication needs. In today's text-crazy world, the medium really is the message. When did the noun *text* also become a verb? WCA (Who cares anyway)! When you text, every character counts. AMOF (As a matter of fact), texting has given rise to a whole new approach to language. BTW (By the way), PAW (parents are watching); BYTM! (Better you than me); KPC (Keeping parents clueless); BBL (Be back later).

The intent with this kind of letter substitution is compression of language and the creation of a code that allows form to follow function. Young people, of course, have always indulged in their own slang, but texting has brought the present slang into the mainstream. Nd hw duz tht mke u feel ?

A culture that cannot read cannot separate illusion from truth; its children are moved by image and slogan rather than the substance of ideas, so they become inherently vulnerable to propaganda. In an illiterate culture, governments lie because they easily can; the language of spin becomes impenetrable when people's language skills decline and their intellectual understanding is at the mercy of emotional manipulation. Opinion and fact become synonyms.

What Computers Can and Can't Do

We use language to make sense of and cope with our world and our lives. Most people admit that technology is influencing how and how much we write. The next step is even more controversial. What if we're able to use computers not only to write but also to read for us? The *New York Times* recently reported that Wall Street traders employ powerful computers to speed-read articles, blog posts, and Tweets, to interpret the words, and then to trade on them. These computers pick up on specific words or phrases and initiate recommendations based on those keys (Darlin, 2011).

What they're doing, however, isn't comprehension. Supercomputers are able only to access and sort through immense quantities of data at lightning speed to produce statistical probabilities based on which words are associated with other words. They don't think about or reflect on what pops up as the best statistical guess: they just do it.

A case in point occurred when a supercomputer named Watson was matched against the two most proficient players on the TV game show *Jeopardy*. Watson defeated both its human challengers and IBM scored a significant public-relations victory. But Watson not only failed to answer a number of questions that the humans correctly answered, it also offered some answers that were ludicrously inaccurate: as far as Watson was concerned, one of the two largest airports in the United States was Pearson International Airport in Toronto, Canada.

In spite of such odd quirks and stumbles, Watson's success on *Jeopardy* became the public launch pad for bigger and better challenges. Watson is now being reprogrammed to assist doctors to analyze vast quantities of medical data to determine a best-guess diagnosis and related treatment. It will undoubtedly also arrive at the correct answer much of the time—except when it doesn't.

Before we ask the computers in our offices, hospitals, schools, and homes to do our reading and thinking for us, we would be well-advised to understand what literacy actually is. Before we accede responsibility for our financial, social, and even physical well being to a *deus ex machina*, we need to examine its potential as a Trojan Horse.

If the Internet is a tsunami, then the computer and all its progeny are the earthquake and aftershocks that created it. They are inextricably linked. Unfortunately, the relentless drive to computerize schools and hook them up intravenously to the Internet continues to confuse form over function.

Whatever the computer can do, it does, and no one questions the fact that function follows form. Computer technology is all-pervasive and mesmerizing precisely because of what computers can do: vast quantities of data are instantly tabulated and manipulated, personal communication is open to every corner of the world, and countless tedious tasks are instantaneously facilitated.

In education, however, form must follow function: the type of learning and the needs of the learner determine the nature of the learning/teaching experience. Before jumping headlong into computer-assisted education, educators need to take a long, hard, critical look at what computers can and can't do.

When they operate as smart pencils or electronic libraries or virtual mailboxes, word processing and information collection and transmission flow naturally from a computer's capabilities. When other types of human needs and computer capabilities interface, however, human experience must first be translated into observable or quantifiable behaviors. In education, curriculum must be translated into discrete items; logically arranged in scope and sequence; interwoven with regular periodic feedback assessment; and supported by similarly structured support materials. In effect, mastery learning, a rigid and limited step-by-step approach to rote learning, has mutated into computer-assisted education.

In this kind of computerized teaching model, a pretest determines an area of weakness or level of expertise. Based on that information, the student is led through a new item of content or is shown a new skill and is then conducted through a practice session. A posttest determines the student's success rate and directs the student either into a remedial exercise or on to the next discrete item or level. The program also presents the teacher with a profile of the student's strengths and weaknesses, a record of the student's progress, a score derived from the student's activities, and homework questions based on the profile.

The process is interactive, efficient, and independent of the teacher. In effect, the computer *is* the teacher. On the surface, this type of educational process appears sound, and, best of all, the computer never has to have a lunch break, never has to be paid, and certainly will never require a pension.

But the danger in allowing the learning/teaching process to be subsumed by the computer is clear: learning is defined by whatever the computer does best. Since computers are best suited to rote learning and objective-style evaluation, students are led through a mastery learning process and rewarded for factual recall and lower-level thinking skills. Since the evaluation system is narrow and mechanical, that's exactly what the curriculum becomes.

Computer-assisted learning programs confine learning to a rigidly controlled, strictly regulated, and carefully managed methodology. Teachers who believe in the second law of teaching will also discover that a lot of computer-assisted learning and evaluation is boring. What computers can't acknowledge or accommodate is how messy much of the human learning process is: how haphazard, unpredictably recursive and individualistic, and inherently egocentric.

What do computers know about and how can they accommodate such factors as an individual student's motivation, background experiences, learning style and exceptionalities, reading proficiency, or mood at any particular moment, or whether or not the student had breakfast that morning? People outside the profession, on the other hand, will say that how and how often computer programs are used to further curricular goals and student needs rests on the judgment and intervention of teachers. They see education in the future as a perfect meld of human and machine: but that synthesis can easily turn into the relentless cyber-organisms we know from science fiction as the Borg.

The more a school board invests in computer technology, the more that technology drives program: accountability demands that the expense be justified. Besides, the technology is endlessly beguiling and hypnotizing: the medium and the message become one.

Curriculum can be articulated in a series of discrete computer-friendly statements; computerized report cards are a few keystrokes away. When the computer-friendly curriculum statements are translated into the teach-test framework of computerized educational programs, classroom teaching and learning, individual student assessment, reporting to parents, and system accountability are instantly harmonized. Computers also facilitate the integration of standardized testing results with individual school- and system-wide accountability. The results are interpreted and reported publicly and are used to rate systems, schools, and teachers: rewards and sanctions based on those results flow naturally, as education and computer technology become synonymous.

But redefining education to fit the limitations of computers has led to disastrous results. From the failure of standardized testing, to the limitations of artificial curricular goals, to the gobbledegook of computerized report-card statements, the focus on computerized education has interfered with the best practices of teaching. A dramatic case in point is the impact of computer programming on the teaching of literacy.

What's so complicated about teaching literacy? Memorize the alphabet, learn to sound out words, answer questions based on the stories you read, complete lessons out of spellers, and learn how to write through prescriptive grammar. Any citizen on the street, given a story anthology, a speller, and a grammar text, should be able to teach students how to read and write. And the best part is you don't even need a teacher at all.

With computerized learning programs based on the content found in hard-copy texts, students can play games that teach them all the basics and, as salespeople are more than happy to point out, since students are having so much fun, they don't even suspect that they're learning. In addition, computer programs keep track of each student's progress and even prepare appropriate comments for the report card. Throw in some oral activities, such as speech arts, and—presto!—you have a literate student fully prepared to get online and ride into the 22nd century. And it's all done for a fraction of the cost of an old-fashioned classroom.

Sound too good to be true? That's because it is. Too many teachers confuse their students' familiarity with electronic technology with mature literacy skills and assume they are proficient readers, or they depend on computerized reading programs to teach the skills of reading for them. In the first instance, being able to access Wikipedia doesn't mean that students can comprehend the entries or discriminate their validity; in the second, computerized reading programs simply replicate the worst kind of reading instruction that has come down through the ages.

Not that you would necessarily notice based on what's going on in some classrooms. In these classrooms, teachers, with or without computers, devote much of their time to assigning and marking work and relatively little time to activities related to explaining and modelling thinking processes; and that's where the individually complex, variable, and messy aspects of higher-level learning take place.

The individual paths leading to insight are unpredictable and varied: the emotional, subjective content of understanding and memory are necessarily intimately personalized, idiosyncratic, and tortuous. Computerized reading instruction, on the other hand, simply apes the most-used reading activities in a non-computerized classroom. With or without the technology, students are mostly involved in recalling, copying, and demonstrating facts: in other words, proving that they've read what they are supposed to be reading.

Reading activities that might touch on the actual complexities of reading comprehension, such as summarizing or synthesizing material, or analyzing an author's style, are seldom incorporated. Students are infrequently asked to reflect thoughtfully on anything they read.

The second law of teaching, in particular, speaks to the task of engaging students in their own learning. Specifically, they should be shown how to focus on their own individual patterns of thought and become aware of how and, eventually, why they process experience the way they do. This ability to consciously reflect on and analyze thinking is termed metacognition, the process that stimulates and enlightens any kind of higher-level learning. In other words, on or off the computer, most teachers are instructing students on playing checkers when they should be teaching the strategies of chess.

Thinking is a messy, individualistic, and language-based business. Humans are constantly testing their personal sense of reality by clarifying, discovering, assessing, reflecting on, resolving, and refining what they really think and feel about experience. We use language to problem-solve in a self-directed individually specific manner, and emotions comprise an essential component in the pathways to meaningful understanding. Far from being an emotion-free intellectual exercise better suited and left to computers, education is actually a multifaceted experience-driven values-based enterprise that can occur only human to human. The three laws of teaching intrinsically recognize and take advantage of that definition.

But try to imagine a modern-day school without computers: you might as well imagine them without students. Computers are here to stay. Some classrooms are already plugged-in environments with students logged on and a teacher's presence merely an e-mail link or an image on a screen. Computers are integrated into every aspect of education: teaching and learning, evaluation, reporting to parents, and administrating schools. They've certainly facilitated and enhanced many aspects of education; but that assistance comes with a price.

A Digital Time Machine

Instead of obsessing on what computers can do, schools need to focus on what computers don't do well or can't do at all. You don't need to be an educator to plug students into a computer and dump them onto the Internet. That's easy. The hard part comes in equipping them with the skills and experiences they'll need to understand and cope with both their virtual and their actual lives. The three laws of teaching are ideal for this task.

Students need to learn the mature skills of speaking, listening, and collaborating in groups; they need to learn how to cope with and reflect on their lives through reading and writing; and they need to understand that important learning may require focused effort, profound determination, and the resilience to learn through trial and error. And when they're personally involved in the learning process, they'll discover how satisfying, interesting, and stimulating learning can be.

The first task, however, is to transform early education by moving forward to the past and replacing computerized activities with experiences in the real world. Computers can't teach young children the attributes of the physical universe: how objects feel, taste, smell, and act. What are the characteristics of water or sand, for example, or what does the number five look and feel like when counted out in buttons or molded in plasticine? With these experiences and so many more, young children need to learn by directly encountering the actual rather than a virtual world.

They also need a real person to listen to their needs: when they're tired or hungry or hurt; when they were yelled at this morning at home or had a fight with their best friend before school; and when they need time to let their wounded feelings heal before they can interact with others or accept the challenge of learning.

Back to the Future: Rerouting Reading

As students grow older and begin to encounter the Internet, they need to expand and enhance a set of skills crucial to their continued development. The paper book may be dead, but the ability to read well is as vital as it ever was. The material students meet on the Internet is often written at an adult or even subject-specialist level; simply comprehending the material requires a full set of independent reading skills.

Effective comprehension also hinges on what an individual brings to the reading; even having enough background information to evaluate the authenticity and validity of a site is a constant concern. As purveyors of computerized reading programs are reluctant to admit, computers may be able to teach children to decode, but they can't teach them to read.

When it comes to reading and writing, however, the importance of computers is taken for granted. More and more, the tasks of teaching students to read and write are being assigned to computer programs. The routine of reading a story and answering questions about it is still the preferred and most common way of teaching reading in schools; and it's the approach that best fits the inherent nature of computers.

By treating reading as a series of right and wrong answers to an arbitrarily selected series of requisite texts, a computer program can package a reading lesson without the intervention of a teacher. The learning can be prescribed in scope and sequence, standardized, computer-directed and evaluated, and summed up with a computer-designated grade. For beginning readers, reading can be separated into its constituent discrete parts and drilled individually, mastered, and then reconstituted into a whole. With computer programs, a phonics approach is advocated, in which students are familiarized with simple graphemes, are led to build them into words, connect the words into phrases and sentences, and then link the sentences into paragraphs. The profile of each student's learning can even be graphed for clarity of understanding. The approach is rigidly controlled and managed and, by definition, accountable.

The only problem with this approach is that it doesn't work. It keeps students busy, it gives each student a mark, and it does nothing to engage students in unravelling the complex system of reading or to foster a love of reading. A computerized approach to reading, instead, guarantees that many children will develop a resistance to, distaste for, and difficulty with the reading process. In simple terms, it bores them to bits.

The question-and-answer approach to teaching reading is arbitrary, repetitious, and unproductive. As Richard Arlington has put it: "Asking questions does little to foster thinking and question answering provides little good evidence of understanding." For reading to flourish in a classroom, it has to be transformed into and appreciated as a dynamic, creative, open-ended, and problem-solving activity.

Reading is reading, whether you're flicking the screen of an e-reader, turning the pages of an old-fashioned printed novel, or unravelling a papyrus scroll. Most students need direction, guidance, and inspiration to help them develop into better and, eventually, confident, fluent, and mature readers. Specific reading practices have been proven over time to be highly effective with students of all ages and abilities (Parsons, 2001). Depending on the grade level taught, the number of prescribed alternative practices, or issues of budget or class size, teachers might be forced to exclude some of these elements. If too many of these elements are missing, however, significant student and teacher frustration with the reading program is inevitable.

As you examine the following effective reading practices, notice that they can all be implemented with or without an electronic component.

An effective reading program should

See Chapter 4, Rediscovering Learning through Personal Response, page 70, for specific methods of implementing this kind of program.

- feature frequent and regular read-alouds by the teacher of both fiction and nonfiction
- include enough reading materials to match individual student interests and abilities
- give students frequent opportunities to select their own reading materials (and not just from a range picked by the teacher)
- allow students regular and significant amounts of in-class time to read (as opposed to answering questions based on their reading)
- incorporate frequent opportunities to respond to materials in a personally significant manner (not just in ways dictated by the teacher or in response to questions posed by the teacher)
- include many opportunities for students to discuss with someone else what they're reading; guide them to seek out and value peer opinions and advice
- be flexible enough to allow students to employ a variety of strategies to comprehend material (e.g., retelling, predicting, relating to personal experience, reflecting, discussing, dramatizing, expanding on the text, comparing, hypothesizing, making inferences and judgments)
- be an integral component of an integrated language arts/English program

Through reading, as with any use of language, we attempt to make sense of and cope with the outside world and our interior reality. But language is never truly objective. Language ignites both an emotional and an intellectual understanding: words, such as *love*, *loss*, *holocaust*, or *faith*, for example, stir our feelings as well as our minds. Personal experience then adds a profound cognitive dimension to any kind of understanding. To an urban child at a zoo, for example, a monkey is a source of wonder and amusement; to a hungry child in the jungle, a monkey is bushmeat.

Our childhood and family experiences, in fact, forge the matrix of beliefs and values against which the content of the outside world is judged and resolved. We construct our understanding of reality on the foundation of our experiences. Is a police officer someone who creates order out of potential chaos, or a symbol of the brutal, arbitrary, and treacherous nature of authority? The understanding obviously depends on the political and cultural context and our experiences within that context.

Just as each pinball in an arcade game can take any number of unpredictable paths through its complex environment until it finally explodes into its final destination, so we each have our own unpredictable, individual, and intuitive pathways to understanding. A particular word or image can trigger an unbidden sequence of arbitrarily juxtaposed memories and emotions that zigzag like chain lightning through our brain's synapses to explode into a moment of unexpected enlightened clarity.

Affective and cognitive behaviors are two inseparable and interdependent sides of the same coin. Our emotions are an intrinsic component of our attempts to comprehend reality. Arising from the bedrock of our beliefs and values, our emotions influence how we prioritize the elements of any experience and how we feel about the experience itself.

For all students, the gateway to intellectual understanding is an appreciation and investigation first of their individual emotional responses. Students need to learn how the feelings invoked by their past and present experiences can be used as entry points into understanding new experiences. They can then intensify the search for meaning by exploring the experiential and emotional connections that any experience evokes.

Students must be guided to reflect thoughtfully on the material they read. They need to develop the ability to consciously reflect on and talk and write about their patterns of thought, how and why they process experience the way that they do.

Forward to the Past: Reflecting on Writing

As with reading, students need to consciously reflect on and talk about their writing, and that means disengaging from the computer and engaging with other human beings. Most teachers use some version of the writer's workshop to teach a process approach to writing. The only trouble is that, except for some lip service paid to collaboration, most of the time the most often-used approach differs little from the ages-old practice of drafting. In this process, students write a rough copy, revise it several times (often with peer assistance), edit and proofread (again, often collaboratively), and hand in a polished final copy for marking. The process is simple and linear. A true writer's workshop approach, however, is far more complex.

We write for the same reason we read: to make sense of and to cope with the world and, ultimately, our place in that world. Writer's workshop refers to a specific approach to organizing the classroom program to reflect and facilitate the process of thinking through writing: the approach includes such components as maintaining a student writing portfolio; collaboration among students for the recursive and blended aspects of composing, revising, and editing; and regular student–teacher conferences. Writing for audiences other than the teacher and frequent sharing and publishing of student writing are also important features.

In the computer age, this process is often truncated. Having the writing product in full view on the monitor and a hard copy only a simple print command away keeps the attention firmly focused on the end point rather than on the thinking processes along the way. Even though the computer is tailor-made for rapid manipulation of text, students tend to neglect revision in favor of editing for surface features. Spell- and grammar- check further encourage this superficial approach.

As well, before the vital act of collaboration can occur, an individual first has to break the hypnotic one-on-one relationship with the computer screen; but the monitor offers a seductive image that is too neat, too cut and dried, to warrant tinkering with. The messy and recursive business of thinking through writing remains at odds with the linear nature of the computer.

Regardless of how the classroom writing program is organized or the number of mandated elements, such as the teaching of prescriptive grammar or certain timetable restrictions, an effective writer's workshop approach will be in place when students are encouraged to

- use writing to explore ideas and think through concepts
- self-select the content and form of their own writing

Answers to the questionnaire on page 53:

1. M
2. R
3. R
4. M
5. R
6. M
7. M
8. R
9. R
10. R

- develop a sense of belonging to a community of writers and appreciate the value of collaboration, at times, for generating and testing ideas and for revising and editing material
- evaluate the effectiveness of their writing, including making decisions about sharing, publishing, and submitting specific pieces for marking

Writing is also hard work. In a point-and-click world, reflection, deliberation, and thoughtful collaboration seem at odds with the virtual reality of immediate gratification. The cold hard truth, however, is that, while computer programs can teach students the mechanics of keyboarding, a computer can't teach anyone to write. Students learn to write by writing.

At the same time, the autonomy of the writer must be balanced by informed and thoughtful input from others. Students need a variety of perspectives from their peers and their teacher at all stages of the writing process to evaluate, remediate, and enhance the effectiveness of their communication. For this kind of program to succeed, however, teachers have to put aside their red pens and take on the challenging task of teaching a process before they ever begin to evaluate a product. The ultimate goal of following the three laws of teaching is developing independent learners. As they develop independence, students can be led to believe in their own self-worth, both as writers and as readers, and to plunge into the personally satisfying enterprise of making sense of their world through literacy.

4

Tackling What's Impossible

The term "impossible" requires a context. For example, schools in the 1960s and '70s experimented with non-graded classrooms, report cards without marks, and schools without interior walls: innovations that seem impossible to consider before or after that particular time period. Even today, outside North America, we can find learning/teaching environments that contrast so drastically with our own way of doing things they are almost impossible to imagine. Use the statements in the box below as a springboard into a discussion of the kinds of "impossible" changes teachers might be able to achieve in their classrooms and their schools.

See page 79 for answers to questionnaire.

Misconception or Research-Based Reality?

Read through the following statements about learning and teaching, and decide which ones are misconceptions (M) and which ones represent practice based on how research reflects the reality of teaching (R).

1. Teaching in Finland is regarded as a higher-prestige profession than being a doctor or a lawyer.   M or R?
2. Finnish teachers spend more time in classrooms than teachers in North America.   M or R?
3. The younger that children start school, the better they will score on international tests.   M or R?
4. The more students are exposed to standardized testing, the better able they are to score well on international testing.   M or R?
5. Merging academic and social objectives makes it harder to achieve either one.   M or R?
6. In some areas of the U.S., Kindergarten children are tested to see if they are gifted.   M or R?
7. High-stakes standardized testing has led to a growing problem of teachers and students cheating.   M or R?
8. Cheating is almost four times greater in charter schools than in regular schools.   M or R?
9. Open education was a philosophy of education that insisted on schools without interior walls.   M or R?
10. Response journals in English/language arts classes are basically student diaries.   M or R?

After doing what's necessary and then what's possible, teachers may be ready to entertain the idea of the impossible. The problem here is that what might be impossible in North America may be what's possible or even necessary somewhere else. In the world beyond North America, other countries have resisted the kinds of practices that infect North American schools. In Finland, for example, education inhabits a totally different universe. Somehow, the Finns have been able to resist the North American siren call of streaming, differentiated instruction, and even standardized testing. Finnish teachers have the latitude to independently follow the three laws of teaching. Their professional responsibilities lead them to individualize their programming, work toward social goals, and maintain their students' self-esteem. What seems impossible to North American teachers is what Finnish teachers regard as the normal course of affairs.

Catching Up with the Finns

The Three Laws of Teaching

1. Teachers must keep their students physically and emotionally safe.
2. Teachers must offer their students interesting and stimulating learning activities.
3. Teachers must keep their students feeling good about how they're learning.

In Finland, classes tend to be small—from 15 to 30 in the lower grades—but there are no minimum or maximum sizes.

These are not the best of times to be a teacher in North America. Cutbacks to education have left schools, by and large, in a state of unsettling disrepair: the curriculum is rigid, politically derived, time-constrained, and age-inappropriate; accountability based on standardized testing has become normalized, while the egalitarian model is fractured; and teachers are well aware that their professionalism, autonomy, salary, and even pensions are under attack.

Now examine the Finnish model for education. Teachers are admired professionals. Teaching, in fact, is considered a higher-prestige profession than being a doctor or a lawyer. As trusted and admired professionals, teachers in Finland expect and receive unparalleled autonomy. In 2011, Rick Salutin, a *Toronto Star* columnist, published a five-part series on education. As part of this series, he offered an intriguing window into teaching in Finland and the differences between teaching in Finland and teaching in North America.

Amazingly enough, Salutin found that Finnish teachers spend the equivalent of four 45-minute classes daily in the middle grades, about half as much as U.S. teachers. Teachers get roughly equal time to do other things, like lesson preparation and marking, working on professional development, or collaborating with their peers. No one questions their dedication or how they use their time, much as we in North America would never question a doctor, lawyer, or an engineer's commitment or autonomy. In fact, Finnish teachers value their sense of professional control and responsibility to the extent that, if they lost that autonomy, they would leave teaching.

And what does the Finnish public get for treating their teachers this way? As well as being a perennial high achiever on Program for International Student Assessment (PISA) tests, Finland also has a high-school graduation rate of 93%, compared to 76% in Canada and 77% in the United States (Salutin, 2011). Since the Organization for Economic Co-operation and Development began ranking countries in 2000 by their scores on PISA tests, Finland scores at or near the top in all categories but does *no* standardized testing till the end of high school.

Finland has accepted that schools must have social as well as academic goals. As North American public schools increasingly attempt to compete with private schools by fracturing their egalitarian model and creating boutique schools, Finland's major educational reform came when they stopped streaming students in academic or vocational directions and created a system designed for greater equality and social unity. As the international testing has proven, the academic and social objectives have gone hand-in-hand and both have been met.

The differences don't end there. In Finland, children don't start school until they are seven years old; preschool starts at six. In North America, few people question the practice of starting children in school as early as possible. In some areas of the U.S., children are even taking standardized tests in Kindergarten to determine if they're gifted. As students grow older and weary of school, we're forced to legislate attendance in high school to combat worrisome dropout rates.

In the March 8, 2012, edition of the *New York Review of Books*, Diane Ravitch wrote an article called "Schools We Can Envy" in which she gave a glowing review for Pasi Sahlberg's *Finnish Lessons: What Can the World Learn from Educational Change in Finland?* Once again, she repudiated everything she once worked for in the U.S. government by holding up the stellar Finnish model against the flawed approach of the United States and other countries around the globe. Since the Finns have demonstrated that their approach is certainly possible, North American teachers can usefully look at their educational system as a model to emulate and a goal to work toward.

Even a more modest set of objectives could revolutionize education in North America. Consider the positive change in schooling if the three laws of teaching were implemented. Imagine the impact on students and their learning if all schools were clean, well-maintained, and abundantly supplied with the latest in learning/teaching resources, electronic and otherwise; if principals and teachers worked collaboratively within a research-based adaptable curriculum; and if teachers were encouraged to be self-motivated, creative, and professionally responsible.

Step Forward, Looking Back

Given the countless constraints most North American teachers encounter on what they teach, how they teach, when they teach, how much time they have to teach a specific concept, and how they go about evaluating the learning, they may think that the only way they can become true professionals is by moving to Finland.

Certainly it's soul-destroying to spend a career following the false trail of improved scores, teaching to the test, living in fear if test results are sub par, and watching impotently as students struggle with a dysfunctional curriculum based on rote learning. On the other hand, everyone has some aspect of their teaching assignment and their professional responsibilities that possesses the potential for growth.

The ultimate goal of any classroom program in any subject area is to help students ultimately become independent, confident, and resourceful learners, individuals who can identify, articulate, explore, and solve their own problems. The key to this kind of development is metacognition.

Metacognition is a term that refers to the ability to consciously reflect on and talk about thinking. Specifically, learners begin to focus on their patterns of thought and become aware of how and, eventually, why they process experiences in the distinct way they do.

This ability is enhanced by developmental factors, such as puberty, and encouraged by reflective practices, such as personal response. Although students can engage in higher-level thinking skills without it, independent, self-motivated learners require metacognitive ability to reach their goals. The most straightforward type of metacognitive reflection involves taking stock of where you are now and where you've come from, and analyzing what you need to do to produce growth or change in your performance. Since children and adolescents are inherently egocentric, developing this kind of objectivity can be difficult. The process may be tentative and recursive, but awareness gradually takes shape.

Rediscovering Learning through Personal Response

Learning is an active, creative process. Most definitions of ideal learners emphasize that they are independent self-motivated individuals who have the ability to find and solve their own problems. By definition, such learners are profoundly aware of their own learning processes.

Learning can, at any one time, incorporate some or all aspects of language. By the same token, the act of processing language involves more than the communicating or recording of our experience. Through language, we construct our sense of reality by revealing, clarifying, discovering, assessing, reflecting on, and refining what we think and feel about experiences.

The learning process combines elements of reading, writing, listening, speaking, observing, doing, and thinking. Through the use of response journals (Parsons, 2001), students can reflect not only on what they've been learning, but also on how and why they learn the way they do. Through a personal-response program in any subject area, they are able to develop the awareness of and, eventually, the commitment to the kind of processes necessary to facilitate and maximize learning. As students become aware of and committed to their own emotional, social, and intellectual growth, the goals of the three laws of teaching are intrinsically satisfied.

In this program, students record, in a variety of formats, their personal reactions to, questions about, and reflections on the following:

- what they read, write, represent, observe, listen to, discuss, do, and think (doing includes such activities as making, performing, calculating, experimenting, manipulating, or creating)
- how they actually go about reading, writing, representing, observing, listening, discussing, or doing

The journal might be a notebook, a folder, a section in a notebook, or an electronic file in a particular subject area. In a rotary timetable, a group of teachers could share a notebook or a personal-response section of a binder, in effect creating an independent study theme across a number of subject areas. On the other hand, a science notebook could have a separate personal-response section devoted solely to that subject. Whatever the arrangement, the only restriction is that students must be aware of the personal-response process and must have some kind of recording routine to accommodate both the process and the evaluation of that process.

In some cases, a journal entry might comprise the entire follow-up to a lesson; in others, the teacher might allot a few minutes at the end of a period to check on students' reactions and make suggestions for other possible reading or projects. Either way, response journal entries provide an invaluable barometer of students' feelings and learning.

Most students remain dependent on the teacher for direction and guidance. They tend to see the function of a reading experience as matching a prescribed set of answers someone else knows to a prescribed set of questions some else devises. They look to the teacher to tell them what to do.

If you ask independent readers to respond to a text in a personally significant way, on the other hand, they possess the confidence, skills, and understanding

Unfortunately, personal response has often been confused with an enforced kind of diary keeping in which students detail what they did the night before, what they had for breakfast, or what rock groups they like best. For further clarification and guidance on this issue, please see the terms *personal diary*, *writer's journal*, *learning logs/work diaries*, or *subject-specific journals* in the glossary (page 87) or read *Response Journals Revisited*, listed in the bibliography.

of the reading process to follow their own idiosyncratic routes through material. Such students require a few model or sample questions to cue their initial efforts. As they gradually develop a better understanding of the different ways in which they can respond in a personally significant manner, they can accept more responsibility for the nature and direction of their responses.

See pages 81 Making a Personal Response and 82 More Cueing Questions for sample questions to cue student responses.

Cueing questions, such as those found in the student guidelines on pages 81 and 82, demonstrate to students how to use their own lives and experiences as springboards into an exploration of material. By self-selecting the question or questions most applicable to their own material and personal leanings, students gain a greater appreciation of what a personal response is all about. The cueing questions act as models on which students will eventually base the formulation of their own questions as they assume their own autonomy in the reading process.

The first guideline, Making a Personal Response (page 81), focuses on a few selected open-ended questions designed to get students started. After their initial efforts, students will be ready for the second, more wide-ranging set of options on page 82.

A Guide to Teacher Reflection

Teachers follow a similar process of personal response as they attempt to inject change into their classroom environments. If they know where they are and where they would like to be, a simple gap analysis will reveal what they need to do to achieve their goals. A wholesale upheaval in their teaching methodology is usually impossible, especially given the many restraints under which they work. But a gradual step-by-step approach to change can be effective and stimulating.

The first step could be a simple exercise in personal reflection based on the three laws of teaching:

1. What did I do today to keep one of my students physically and emotionally safe? How can I do even more tomorrow?
2. What learning activities did I offer my students to do today that they found interesting and stimulating? What can I do tomorrow?
3. What did I do today to keep my students feeling good about how they're learning? What can I do tomorrow?

See page 83 A Checklist of Classroom Possibles for tool for teacher reflections.

This kind of reflection can transform how teachers feel about themselves as professionals and reenergize their approach to their students and their students' learning. A small step can make a significant difference. See page 83 for A Checklist of Classroom Possibles. Using it, teachers can determine which steps they can and want to take; which ones they can take immediately; and which ones they'll have to reserve for some time in the future. This checklist has relevance for a range of subject areas.

For teachers trying to expand their classroom programs, however, the critical component is the one they often have little control over and that affects all aspects of their professional lives: evaluation.

The Shrinking Curriculum

Evaluation, specifically standardized testing, is the roadblock that currently makes moving from the necessary in teaching to the possible—or even entertaining the feasibility of the impossible—problematic. The sanctions involved in standardized testing are even challenging some teachers' moral judgment. Since many teachers believe that the results of standardized testing reflect socioeconomic factors and not their own expertise, they feel backed into a corner. With accountability tied to testing, teachers and schools are motivated to teach to the test and fudge results whenever possible. As W. C. Fields once said, "A thing worth having is a thing worth cheating for."

In 2009, for example, 178 educators in the Atlanta public schools system erased and changed student answers to increase scores on standardized tests. "A culture of fear, intimidation, and retaliation permeated the Atlanta Public Schools system from the highest ranks down," revealed the Georgia Bureau of Investigation in its scathing report. In the 56 schools investigated, 44 were found culpable. (*Toronto Star*, July 8, 2011)

The United States isn't alone in discovering that high-stakes testing leads to "irregularities" in the schools being tested. The testing agency in Ontario, Canada, threw out three years of results from a London-area middle school when an investigation revealed "puzzling irregularities" in student responses and "erasings," among other irregularities. The previous year, by the way, the school principal was named one of the country's 32 outstanding principals. (*Toronto Star*, August 11, 2011)

Without doing any onsite investigation, the authors of *Freakonomics* discovered statistically that about 5% of teachers actually changed their students' answers or filled in any question left blank after the test was completed (Levitt & Dubnew, 2006: chapter 1). What the authors couldn't discover was the number of teachers who cheated in subtler ways, such as giving their students more than the allotted time, hinting at correct answers, or even practicing parts of the test ahead of time. But the authors do cite a North Carolina study in which 35% of teacher respondents stated that they had witnessed a colleague cheating on standardized tests.

Other teachers are engaged in a variety of questionable classroom activities that don't qualify as cheating but subvert the intent of testing. These attempts to raise classroom scores include making the previous year's test a key component of the current year's teaching and drilling students on a regular basis on similar kinds of tests to the detriment of the curriculum.

Students themselves are certainly not immune to the pressures of high-stakes testing. The *Dallas Morning News* found evidence that tens of thousands of students cheated every year without being detected, especially on the 11th-grade tests required for graduation. Cheating was almost four times greater in charter schools than in traditional high schools (Benton, 2007). Students can buy essays from websites and even specify the grade they'd like to get: universities, in turn, secure the services of other websites to electronically check essays for plagiarism.

Needless to say, principals of individual schools and school-board administrators are also susceptible to the pressures of raising student scores. How many browbeat and harass teachers with poorly performing students, attempt to alter results by excusing students who they know will not test well, or even alter or disguise the results?

When you add in the uneven playing field that handicaps many students before they even take the test, all the questionable practices surrounding standardized testing, and the out-and-out cheating, the only certainty about the results from standardized testing is that they're critically flawed and they do nothing to improve learning. For teachers attempting to adhere to the three laws of teaching, standardized testing is a huge roadblock.

Expanding Evaluation to Meet the Needs of the Learner

To ensure success with the possibles of education and to have any chance of reaching some of the impossibles, teachers have to design classroom evaluation systems that offset some of the negative effects of standardized testing. The place to start is with the kinds of evaluative practices that meet the needs of the learner.

Evaluation has a profound impact on all aspects of the learning/teaching process. As well as assessing student progress and achievement, and program effectiveness, evaluation also influences a student's perception of learning, as well as his or her commitment to and involvement with the goals of the program. In order to contribute to the aims and objectives of the learning/teaching environment, evaluation must meet the needs of the learner.

Students are constantly being tested by someone else in ways beyond the students' control and for purposes not of the students' choosing. Students are constantly being acted upon by evaluation without a clear sense of why or how it helps them to become independent self-reliant learners. Instead, their learning is constantly being branded with letters and numbers that bear no relationship to how they're attempting to grow as individuals.

In a perfect world, everyone involved with students would understand and help to facilitate the true aim of all evaluation: self-evaluation. In this case, teachers would begin quite early to prepare students to comprehend their active role in the learning process and the purpose and benefits of evaluation.

As students gain maturity and practice, self-evaluation can be used more and more. The more that teachers can arrange meaningful situations in which students can practice this ability, the more adept students will become in applying self-evaluation. Ideally, a steady progression should be developed from criteria generated by the teacher toward criteria generated by the students. Clearly, a high degree of knowledge, expertise, and commitment is vital if a teacher hopes to implement this kind of program.

Without this element of self-evaluation, curriculum truly does shrink to the boundaries of evaluation. Students become conditioned to work for grades and to depend on only external criteria. They work simply to complete the assignment or course and evaluate their success by the grade awarded, rather than the effects of permanent learning. If tests and grades are the only outcomes, many possibilities for meaningful learning will be ignored. Regardless of how interesting and stimulating an activity might be, a teacher will inevitably hear a chorus of "Does this count?" If it doesn't, students immediately disengage; if it does, they immediately try to find the easiest and best way to bet a good mark.

But self-evaluation takes a long time to master. An evaluation system can first be broadened, step by step, in any number of ways before self-evaluation is gradually introduced. Teachers first need to assess the age, maturity, experience, and readiness of their students before deciding on which approach might be successful.

See page 85 A Checklist of Possibles for Evaluation for a tool to aid in effective evaluation.

In the checklist on page 85, teachers can determine which steps they can and want to take; which ones they can take immediately; and which ones they'll have to reserve for some time in the future.

Values in a Hypocritical World

Students don't walk into a school empty-handed or empty-headed. They carry with them all the experiences and influences from their world that have shaped their values up to that point. Their sports heroes have taught them that winning is the only thing that counts; that using performance-enhancing drugs in the pursuit of dominance is a necessary evil; and that racial and homophobic slurs are the common currency of athletic competition.

Their music idols have tutored them about "ho's", "fags", and "attitude"; indoctrinated them on the glories of conspicuous material consumption; and even enlightened them on the name of the preferred champagne. The Internet, gaming, and social networking have created a virtual reality contaminated with themes of sexual exploitation, violence, and conformity, intertwined with the imperatives of commercial gain. Celebrities from all walks of life, including politicians, have exemplified the pervasiveness of hypocrisy, lying, promiscuity, and greed. The wars that form the backdrop of students' lives have produced a confusing fog of cultural, racial, and religious intolerance.

And at the core of their beings rest all the values, good and bad, modelled by their parents and guardians since the day of their birth. Add in all the insecurities, vulnerabilities, disappointments, fears, and partially formed dreams and aspirations that pick away at their objectivity, and you have the ingredients for a jumbled value stew and a recipe for bullying. This motley collection also produces an atmosphere inimical to the goals of the three laws of teaching.

The virtual world of the Internet contributes to and magnifies students' precarious and uncertain moral sense. With computers so ubiquitous and students' skills assumed, too often, to be more sophisticated than they actually are, students are ill-equipped and ill-prepared for the inherent challenges of the Internet. As a result, they begin the formidable and daunting task of surfing the Internet without first learning the basic skills necessary to survive.

Too many students get stalled before they even get started. A simple search often produces hundreds if not thousands of sites: too much information and too many choices. Few students possess the criteria for evaluating the usefulness of one site over another. Instead of skimming, scanning, and productively discriminating among text and images, they often let their gaming instinct to point and click take over. As a result of their lack of skills, students allow non-thinking activities, such as copying and printing articles and images, to take precedence over understanding. Plagiarism becomes a way of life. Students download and print material without change or with little comprehension and claim it as their own.

The Internet is also an irresistible combination of flea market, commercial mall, entertainment complex, fairground sideshow, and social playground. Too many entrepreneurs, legitimate and otherwise, are shilling for too many services and products. The computer screen is alive with the latest in electronic come-ons and promises. No wonder students have such difficulty staying online and on task when they're doing research. Too many distractions unrelated to their search are merely a click away.

Students need to learn that values underlie everything they do or say or think. How they behave on the Internet, for instance, is simply an extension of how they behave in their homes, schools, or schoolyards. People who lie, cheat, steal, and bully undermine the communities in which they live and the work and happiness of those around them. While it may not always be easy, matching actions to beliefs is vital to personal and societal well-being.

Values lie at the heart of the learning/teaching process; they are the Rosetta Stone by which we learn how to interpret the nature of our world and the mystery of our lives. Our values govern how we behave in our personal and professional relationships and provide a yardstick for measuring the satisfactions and rewards that stem from our actions. Our values, consequently, determine the success or failure of teachers attempting to implement the three laws of teaching. The inculcation of society's values must be the fundamental work of schools. But what values might those be?

We seem to have a contradictory, almost bipolar, approach to values: those we say we aspire to and those we actually live by. We say we believe in cooperation for the good of all as exemplified by collaborative team-building and problem-solving; in the real world, we reward aggression, competitiveness, and individual achievement. We hold honesty to be the solid core of all our relationships; yet lies and half-truths are accepted as the currency of politics and the business and corporate worlds. We believe that a civil society should protect and support those most vulnerable; meanwhile, we neglect the needs of the very young, the very old, the poor, and the powerless.

As students learn more and more about their world, they realize that a moral canyon separates what people say and what they do. Countries take advantage of other countries that are economically, politically, or militarily vulnerable. The corporate imperatives of profit and loss override the requisites of basic health, education, and social welfare systems. Religious values are tainted as the world's religions vie for moral pre-eminence, with their extreme elements resorting to bigotry, violence, and terror.

Meanwhile, democratic values are routinely debased during the no-holds-barred cutthroat competitions that we call elections. The winners get to pursue their narrow, self-serving, partisan agendas while the losers lick their wounds and plot their revenge. Any sense that we elect leaders to govern the country in the best interests of the entire population is naïve and old-fashioned. To the victors belong the spoils.

What does justice mean when Wall Street greed precipitates a worldwide recession and governments reward their rapacity with colossal bailouts? To make matters worse, the debt is then transferred onto ordinary citizens by implementing austerity programs, by attacking public-service salaries, health care, and pensions, and by instituting more cutbacks to the social safety net. In the 1987 film *Wall Street*, Gordon Gecko intoned the phrase "Greed is good." In 1987, the audience regarded the sentiment as contemptible: looking back, that sentiment seems eerily prophetic.

In this age of spin, double-speak, and hypocrisy, why are we surprised that our young people are morally confused? Racist, sexist, and homophobic values commonly riddle the music they listen to, the music videos they watch, and the violent video games they play. In the virtual reality of plugged-in wrap-around electronic lifestyles, instant fame is a single YouTube moment away. Values are compromised in the Internet chat rooms and adult websites they visit and are dissipated in the ephemeral lure of an impersonal keystroke.

In the midst of this contradictory miasma, students also become aware of the power of physical attractiveness, celebrity, wealth, political influence, physical prowess, privileged occupations, and the majority culture. They intuit that people with power don't seem to be bound by the same prosocial rules as everyone else:

fits of temper, self-centredness, social excesses, and aggression are routinely practiced by the powerful and excused by everyone else.

Revitalizing Values

There's no great secret involved in revitalizing the learning/teaching process or in developing an effective anti-bullying program. It doesn't cost much money and can be implemented at any level and in any school. The foundation of the learning/teaching process and the core of any anti-bullying policy is the same: cooperation for the good of all and respect for self, peers, and adults. With these values firmly in place, schools become welcoming environments in which students feel physically and emotionally safe; students trust that teachers will give them interesting and stimulating things to do and accept wholeheartedly the challenges of the learning experiences; and everyone feels good about themselves and about each other—including the teacher.

Teachers can make a critical difference in how students perceive their world but routinely let themselves off the hook by claiming that schools can't change society; schools can, however, change students and students can eventually promote change. School leaders have a crucial choice to make: either they allow their schools to passively reflect the relativism of the larger society or they proactively envelop students in an equity-based environment. In the former case, learning is narrowed to numbers on a standardized test; teachers and students waste their time together fervently pursuing accountability like greyhounds chasing a mechanical rabbit. No matter how they train or practice or even cheat, at the end of each term, they're back at the starting gate chasing the same unrealizable target.

With a value-based curriculum, on the other hand, success is a predictable by-product of an effective learning/teaching environment. Learning is inherently maximized when students feel physically and psychologically safe, appreciated by peers and adults, and eager to take risks when challenged in their studies.

Teachers must be held accountable in this environment—but that accountability must not be based on a mindless punishment-and-reward system derived from arbitrary class or school rankings. Certain basic values have to be recognized, implemented, and respected by everyone in a school, including administration, teachers, office staff, and visiting parents or guardians. If anyone, including the principal, undercuts or neglects those values, they must freely conform to the standard or leave the school.

Like it or not, to make any kind of dent in the melange of influences that persuade students as they develop a personal ethical code, teachers have to lead by example. Values are caught, not taught. The most important subject in the curriculum is the teacher: every moment of every day, teachers must exemplify what it means to be a caring, responsible, and decent human being.

The Problem with Change from the Top Down

Most teachers recognize the importance of reflective practice, renewal through change, and adaptable methodology. The central problem with applying this kind of professional autonomy is the rigidity and resistance to change of any institution, including boards of education. Besides, teachers also feel that administration and office staff have the time and expertise to examine competing theories of pedagogy that classroom teachers don't. They wait for change to be initiated from the top down.

In the past, however, when change was initiated from the top without the understanding, leadership, and acceptance of teachers, these initiatives failed. In Ontario, for example, during the 1960s and '70s, the vision from the top of the educational hierarchy was progressively radical and completely open-ended. Here's what some of those educators were daring to talk about:

- In 1966, Ontario Education Minister William Davis, commenting on the fact that some boards of education were experimenting with ungraded elementary classrooms, said, "It may be unrealistic to apply grade levels since some children learn and progress faster than others."
- In that same year, Dr. F.W. Minkler, the Director of Education for the North York Board of Education, declared that "the days are gone when youngsters are held back for lack of making progress. The emphasis today is on youngsters developing rather than mastering a set curriculum."
- Again in 1966, Toronto elementary schools implemented new report cards with no marks at all, only teacher anecdotal comments. Barry Lowes, the chairman of the school board, also promoted less homework. "High school students are coming home and doing 3½ hours homework. This is ridiculous," he declared. "They can't have a life of their own."
- In January 1969, year-round schooling was proposed for Toronto's 115,000 high-school students.

During those years, administrators attempted to change the fundamental principles of education and implement an innovative curriculum and methodology. Based on comprehensive learning/teaching theories and supported by scientific research, the principle that all children *can* learn became the cornerstone of the curriculum. Thoroughly egalitarian, schools were expected to stimulate, guide, support, nurture, and remediate learning in the individual child.

Since the basic principles of learning dictated the means, a wide variety of paths were opened through a negotiated syllabus. Classrooms were required to be child-centred and activity oriented. Theory and practice became inseparable: process and product were balanced. Society served the rights of the child and all children had the right to learn and succeed.

As always with change in a top-down model, however, implementation proved to be extremely difficult. Introducing these kinds of profound changes, in fact, was a bit like trying to turn an ocean liner on a dime: the captain spins the wheel and declares that we're all headed in the opposite direction. Meanwhile, the ship has barely budged.

In Ontario, at this time, administrators demanded immediate change while most teachers were left with their heads spinning and their eyes on traditional goals. Needless to say, administrators and teachers immediately clashed.

Given their training and traditions, teachers at that time were understandably reluctant to jump headlong into this new vision for education. Historically, they were an intrinsic part of a product-oriented system based on the mastery, primarily by means of rote learning and memorization, of a prescribed syllabus. Students all followed a single path through a non-negotiable curriculum. Indeed, schools were considered cultural-literacy gymnasia in which students were expected to prove their mettle in the cauldron of learning. Although only a small percentage of the student population ever attained a post-secondary degree, all students were sorted out through the educational process and deposited in their "appropriate" place in society.

The gap between what most teachers believed and how they taught and the new beliefs and methods they were expected to surrender to was a chasm. The new curriculum and the innovative methodology required comprehensively reworked curriculum documents; an infusion of complementary classroom equipment, texts, and other resource materials; a radically different set of teaching skills; and an altered approach to reporting to parents.

This Herculean and complex task of implementing change immediately encountered disabling obstacles. The implementation model itself was a disaster from the beginning: teachers were expected to comply with new guidelines while or even before they had been in-serviced on what was expected. Meanwhile, implementation occurred on a trial-and-error basis: mostly error, as it turned out.

No one at that time appreciated how pervasive and powerful a school's dominant teaching culture was. If a curriculum expert came into a school to explain and leave behind new guidelines and resource documents, the instructional binders began to gather dust before the expert even left the building. If you took teachers out of their schools for a day or two of instruction in the new guidelines and techniques, they would revert to the old ways once they returned to their home buildings.

Boards tried removing a few teachers from a school, in-servicing them in a more comprehensive and in-depth manner, and sending them back to in-service their colleagues. The hope was that these lead teachers would have more credibility with their staffs than outside experts. The reality was that even these teachers were inevitably subsumed by the dominant school culture when they returned. Even when a team of teachers from the same grade level or subject area were removed for exhaustive training, they would usually encounter conflict within their group and with the staff as a whole. The fact that no one was able to solve the problems of implementation ensured that the educational ocean liner never really changed course.

There were some exceptions. In these pockets of brilliance, teachers thoroughly understood the new pedagogy, believed in the approach, and had the courage and talent to implement what they believed. When an entire school willingly embraced the new philosophy, the results were transformational.

Closing Down Open Education

This attempt to revolutionize education finally came to a stuttering and acrimonious halt when someone in North America confused an idea with a wall.

Open education was a philosophy of education that arose in the 1970s, modelled after British primary programs. These classrooms integrated learning tasks with play, encouraged cooperative learning over competition, and de-emphasized rote learning of all kinds. Ideally, learning activities grew out of the individual interests and needs of the students and could be conducted in any classroom regardless of configuration.

In North America, this philosophy was unfortunately confused with an open-classroom approach to education, in which interior classroom walls were removed and teachers carried on in the large open spaces as they would have in their individual classrooms.

The fact that open classrooms soon disappeared surprised no one, especially teachers. They hated them. When teachers as different from each other in philosophy and methodology as apples and carrots were thrown into the same physical teaching space, chaos quickly ensued. It didn't help that the public and many teachers began to equate open education with a laissez-faire kind of "do your own thing." To no one's surprise and to the relief of traditional teachers, slowly but surely, the walls came creeping back up again.

The fact that open education was mistakenly tarred with the same brush as open classrooms was a tragedy for meaningful learning and teaching, especially in the primary grades. By and large, students who believed they experienced open education probably didn't. Everybody talked a good game about the approaches that administrators were demanding but, once the classroom doors were closed, most teachers mostly carried on as they always had—with some important exceptions.

Getting Back to Learning

Answers to the questionnaire on page 67:

1. R
2. M
3. M
4. M
5. M
6. R
7. R
8. R
9. M
10. M

Educators in the 1960s and 1970s dreamed big and aimed high. Even though most schools fell short of their whole transformational vision, the ethos in schools did change in profound ways. The civil rights and feminist movements, for example, were reflected in the values promoted in schools. School staffs were expected to provide an environment free of sexist, racial, cultural, and ability-related stereotyping. (The goal to fight homophobic stereotyping, on the other hand, was still many years away.)

Since the educational model was egalitarian and geared toward the individual, teachers were expected to display a respectful attitude toward all students and a genuine regard for their learning. By the same token, teachers were acquiring a new-found sense of professionalism that demanded respect from colleagues and parents alike and that evolved into a self-imposed sense of professional responsibility and accountability. As a result, collaboration among adults in a school and among students in a classroom became an expected everyday occurrence. Teachers expected to be meaningfully involved in the decision-making and problem-solving processes on a schoolwide basis. They had input on whatever was going on in their schools, from budgetary matters to scheduling to curricular implementation projects. In this collegial atmosphere, the role of the principal changed from boss of the school to first among equals.

This collaborative approach was expressed at the classroom level with the introduction of cooperative learning strategies. Students were taught how to work productively in groups for the benefit of all. They were also given opportunities to collaboratively make decisions and solve problems related to the classroom learning experience, much as their teachers were doing in the school as whole.

Certain truths about education were also widely held to be self-evident:

- Education is a lifelong process; schools should reflect and accommodate that belief.
- All students have the right to learn and progress to the best of their abilities; since children are different from each other, these differences should be reflected in classroom practice (in other words, teachers should individualize their programs to the best of their abilities).

- Play was acknowledged to be children's work; activity-based child-centred primary programs were expected to be play-based.

Different teachers, of course, had different ideas about how or even whether these goals could be accomplished, but the basic principles were accepted as the theoretical foundation of a school's mandate. Regardless of their personal beliefs, however, teachers regarded themselves as the beginning and end of whatever happened in their classrooms. When central office sent down a new policy or program directive, teachers accepted the responsibility of evaluating the efficacy of that change before they would implement it. The well-being of their charges gave teachers the authority to lead.

Inspirational Indian leader Gandhi was once being interviewed by a journalist when a stream of people swept past outside the window. Gandhi immediately got up to leave. When he was asked, "Where are you going?" he answered, "There go my people; I must run to catch up to them for I am their leader." He understood that meaningful and lasting change comes from the bottom up, and that true leaders must be ready to accept and capitalize on the next inevitable evolution.

And so it is with teaching. Maybe it's time to work backwards in education and, in the process, allow teachers to discover rebirth as professionals. If we start from the ground up, we can establish the kind of classroom environment in which all children should learn and let the professionals take responsibility for how that happens. In that kind of environment, schools would be constantly filled with a lively and energizing debate about pedagogy and about how to enable all students to achieve to the best of their abilities and to acquire the knowledge, skills, and values they need to become responsible members of a democratic society.

Starting from the ground up means professionals have specific responsibilities that trump whatever obstacles are placed in their paths:

1. They must keep their students physically and emotionally safe.
2. They must give their students interesting and stimulating things to do.
3. They must keep their students feeling good about themselves.

Schools do not hold a monopoly on learning. Learning begins before the age of schooling and continues long after schools are left behind. Schools will remain relevant to the needs of a society only if they reflect and serve the needs of such learners; if they can indeed move from the necessary to the possible and, perhaps some day, to the impossible; if their teachers understand and invoke three basic principles that can transform classroom environments. Our children deserve no less.

Making a Personal Response

As people read, they think about what's happening in a book in many different ways. Sometimes, questions spring to their minds about some of the characters and how they are behaving. At other times, readers might be impressed by the way someone or something is described. They might even be reminded of something similar that happened to them or someone they know.

After reading independently today, try to describe the kinds of impressions that your reading has inspired and note any questions that come to mind. You might find the following questions useful in forming your responses. Bear in mind that they are only suggestions. If you have a better way to write about your reading experience, feel free to follow your own path.

- After reading this far, what more do you hope to learn about what these characters plan to do, what they think, feel, and believe, or what happens to them?

- As you think ahead to your next day's reading, what possible directions might the story take? How do you hope the story will unfold?

- If the setting and characters were changed to reflect your own neighborhood and your own friends and acquaintances, how would the events of the story have to change and why would that be so?

- Do you wish that your own life was more like the lives of the people in the story you're reading or that the people you know were more like those in the story? In what ways would you like the real world to be more like the world of your book? In what ways are you glad that they're different?

Pembroke Publishers ©2012 *Back to Learning* by Les Parsons ISBN 978-1-55138-281-4

More Cueing Questions

You might have found that the first list of cueing questions didn't quite fit the book you were reading or what you wanted to say about it. The following questions give you more choice. Keep in mind that, when you're ready, you can devise your own questions and write about your reading in your own way. The following questions are suggestions only and are intended for students who choose to use them.

- As you think ahead to your next day's reading, what possible directions might the story take? How do you hope the story will unfold? Why?

- What surprised you about the section you read today? How does this change affect what might happen next in the story?

- As you read today, what feelings did you experience in response to events or characters (e.g., irritation, wonder, disbelief, recognition, dislike) and why do you think you felt this way?

- What questions do you hope to have answered as you read more of the story?

- What startling/unusual/effective words, phrases, expressions, or images did you come across in your reading today? Which ones would you like to have explained or clarified? Which ones would you like to use in your own writing?

- Have you ever had a dream or daydream that seemed similar to an event or theme in this book? Try to describe the dream or daydream and trace the parallels.

- After reading this far, what more do you hope to learn about what these characters plan to do, what they think, feel, and believe, or what happens to them?

- With what characters do you most closely identify? For which characters do you feel the most sympathy for? What is it about these characters that make you feel this way?

- How much do you personally agree or disagree with the way various characters think and act, and the kinds of beliefs and values they hold? Where do you differ and why?

- What issues in this story are similar to real-life issues that you've thought about or had some kind of experience with? How has the story clarified, confused, or changed your views on any of these issues?

- What characters and situations in the story remind you of characters and situations in your own life? How are they similar and how do they differ?

- How did the characters or events in this book remind you of characters or events in other books you've read or movies or TV shows you've seen? Do you prefer one of these treatments over the others? If so, why?

Pembroke Publishers ©2012 *Back to Learning* by Les Parsons ISBN 978-1-55138-281-4

A Checklist of Classroom Possibles

How can I encourage discussions that cover a range of comprehension/thinking skills?

❑ relating to personal experience

❑ hypothesizing

❑ understanding cause and effect

❑ recognizing central meaning

❑ predicting

❑ making inferences

❑ comparing

❑ distinguishing fact from opinion

❑ recalling details

❑ making judgments

❑ expanding on the text

How can I introduce more opportunities for my students to broaden their use of listening and speaking skills?

❑ discussing

❑ asking questions

❑ answering questions

❑ solving problems

❑ reporting

❑ interviewing

❑ giving directions

❑ dramatizing situations

❑ storytelling

❑ collaborating in small groups

How can I help my students refine their problem-solving focus?

❑ by being a responsive and interested listener

❑ by asking questions to elicit details, expansion and addition of ideas, clarification

❑ by not asking questions to which I already know the answers

Pembroke Publishers ©2012 *Back to Learning* by Les Parsons ISBN 978-1-55138-281-4

How can I introduce situations that will allow my students to extend their uses of language?

❑ thinking and talking about how and what they learn

❑ reflecting

❑ predicting

❑ clarifying

❑ explaining

❑ imagining

❑ role-playing

❑ reasoning

❑ justifying

❑ arguing

How can I develop a program that will improve students' reading and writing skills?

❑ by letting them see me reading and writing for different purposes

❑ by introducing student–teacher and student–student reading and writing conferences

❑ by reading aloud both fiction and nonfiction to them on a regular basis

❑ by making sure they have enough variety of reading material to match their individual interests, reading levels, and prior experiences

❑ by setting different purposes for reading: enjoyment, pursuing personal interests, investigation, solving problems

❑ by using a writer's workshop approach to writing

❑ by completing myself some of the written tasks I set for them and sharing the results with them

Pembroke Publishers ©2012 *Back to Learning* by Les Parsons ISBN 978-1-55138-281-4

A Checklist of Possibles for Evaluation

How I can acknowledge the difference in intent between formative and summative evaluation?

❑ by ensuring that evaluation is an ongoing daily process that regularly focuses on formative growth

❑ by differentiating for the students when I am acting as a trusted adult or mentor and when I am acting as teacher/evaluator

❑ by distinguishing and maintaining a balance between record-keeping for report-card purposes and observations that focus on a student's individual needs and growth

How I can match the form of evaluation to the task, the kind of learning, and stage of learning?

❑ by making use of self- and peer-evaluative techniques, such as response journals and peer conferencing

❑ by using a variety of methods to gather data including

- Work diaries/learning logs, subject-specific journals, response journals

- Performance evaluations (such as completing experiments, role-playing, presentations, demonstration of skills)

- Teacher–student conferences

- Writing folders

- Questionnaires

- Observations

GLOSSARY

The definitions in this selected glossary reflect the meanings that are used in the text.

achievement: the attainment of specific learning goals in a school setting

affective: a term from psychology referring to emotional activity.

aggression: subjugating someone through an unfair or irrational use of power

at risk: a descriptor applied to students with academic, emotional, or social difficulties, or a combination of these difficulties, serious enough to jeopardize acceptable progress in school

biphobia: aversion toward bisexuality and bisexual people as a group or as individuals

brainstorming: generating a list of examples, ideas, or questions to illustrate, expand on, or explore a central idea or topic

bully: someone who uses an imbalance of power to repeatedly aggress against and harm another through physical, emotional, or social means

bystander: someone who witnesses someone bully another

cognitive: a term from psychology referring to intellectual activity

collaboration: problem solving in pairs and in other small groups (see also *cooperative learning*)

conflict resolution: an in-school process using peer mediators to resolve conflicts between and among students

control disorders: clinical conditions suffered by students who are unable to consistently monitor and regulate their own behavior

cooperative learning: a variety of small-group instructional techniques focusing on peer collaboration

curriculum: at one time, a synonym for syllabus; the current definition, which reflects the complexity of learning, refers to everything that happens in a school

cyberbullying: using the communication capacities of computers to bully others

detention: a form of punishment in a school in which an individual is detained and confined in a specific location during the school day

discipline: the practice of establishing correct order and behavior in a classroom using such methods as rules, direct instruction, and punishment

drama in education: involves all students in the classroom in spontaneous, unscripted, unrehearsed activities; no audience is present

ethnocultural: identifying with a group of people sharing a heritage ancestry as well as other characteristics, which might include physical, cultural, linguistic, or religious components

evaluation: determining progress toward and attainment of specific goals; assessing student progress and achievement as well as program effectiveness

exceptionalities: physical, intellectual, social, and emotional characteristics that mark an individual as significantly different from the norm; the difference may signal either gifted or deficient development

gay: a term generally accepted to refer to both male and female homosexuals, but which is often used to denote males alone

homophobia: an active hatred of, dislike of, or discomfort with people who are not heterosexual; homophobia includes prejudice, discrimination, harassment, and acts of violence brought on by fear or hatred

homosexuality: a sexual orientation in which a person feels physically sexually attracted to people of the same gender

instruction: the established plan of actions and content specifically chosen to enable learning

learning logs/work diaries: day-to-day written records of what is done in a particular subject area and what and how students are learning; commonly used when students are working independently for extended periods, such as on projects or experiments

lesbian: a contemporary term denoting female homosexuals

literacy: the ability to read and write; often extended today to include the processing of information from all sources and systems, including electronic and micro-electronic

literature: writing of high quality and significance because of a successful integration of such components as style, organization, language, and theme

media literacy: the ability to analyze and reflect on the ways in which media events are formulated and how they function

mentor: a trusted and accomplished person who takes a personal and direct interest in the development and education of another

modelling: the act of serving as an example of behavior; for example, when a teacher displays a genuine courtesy toward others and a respect for individual differences

personal diary: daily, spontaneous private writing; teachers do not read it unless given permission by the student; such writing grew out of the practice of daily "free" writing, or writing for the sake of writing; adopted by English/language arts teachers to develop the habit of daily writing

prosocial: a term from psychology that designates behavior that conforms to the generally accepted rules of social interaction and personal and property rights

Queen Bee (popularized in the book *Queen Bees and Wannabes* by Rosalind Wiseman): the dominant leader of a female clique

read-alouds: any material read aloud, often by the teacher; can be fiction or non-fiction

relationship bullying: employing such methods as rumors, name-calling, cliques, and exclusion to bully

response journal: a notebook, folder, section of a notebook, or electronic file in which students record their personal reactions to, questions about, and reflections on what they read, view, write, represent, observe, listen to, discuss, do and think, and how they go about these processes; first used extensively in English/language arts programs; can be adapted to any unit of study in any subject area

risk-taking: the internalized understanding that mistakes and approximations are good; the freedom to experiment, extend the known, or try something new without unduly worrying about failing or being wrong

same-sex: a term coined to refer to a context in which one gender is involved, as in *same-sex marriage*

sexual harassment: sexual behavior that a reasonable person should have known was unwanted or likely to be unwanted and distressing

sexual orientation: a person's emotional, physical, and sexual attraction and the expression of that attraction

standardized test: a test with established norms to enable comparisons; for example, the Stanford-Binet Intelligence Scale

stereotyping: to hold a commonly held view, often simplified and rigid, of the characteristics of groups of people

subject-specific journals: a record similar to a log or work diary, but including additional information about how students feel about what they're doing, as well as a formative self-evaluation component; these grew out of the recognition of the importance of metacognition in learning but without the reliance on personal response; can be applied to any subject area

target: the object of a bully's aggression

transphobia: a range of negative attitudes and feelings toward transsexual or transgender people

Tribes: a prepackaged program involving a year-long series of lessons designed to increase prosocial behaviors and teach cooperative learning skills

writer's journal: carried and maintained by choice, a source book for writing random jottings made at home or school; its use grew out of the writer's workshop approach to creative writing; valued as a method of extracting first-draft material from everyday life

SELECTED BIBLIOGRAPHY

Associated Press/MTV (2011) *AP-MTV digital abuse*, September 27, 2011; at surveys.ap.org

Association for Childhood Education International (2009) *Report*.

Benton, Joshua, *Dallas Morning News*, June 4, 2007.

Bronson, Po and Merryman, Ashley (2009) *NurtureShock*. New York, NY: Hachette Book Group

Coates, Ken S. and Morrison, Bill (2011) *Campus Confidential: 100 startling things you don't know about Canadian universities*. Toronto, ON: James Lorimer & Company Ltd.

Consumer Reports (2011) "7.5 million Facebook users are under the age of 13, violating the site's terms"; at http://pressroom.consumerreports.org/pressroom/2011/05/consumer-reports-survey-75-million-facebook-users-are-under-the-age-of-13-violating-the-sites-terms.html

Corporate Voices for Working Families *Public Policy Strategies to Improve Workforce Readiness*, November 2008; at www.cvworkingfamilies.org

Darlin, Damon "Lens" *New York Times*, January 2, 2011.

Dishon, Dee, and Pat Wilson O'Leary (1998) *Guidebook for Cooperative Learning: Techniques for Creating More Effective Schools*. 3rd ed. Holmes Beach, Fl: Learning Publications.

Dyer, Gwynne (2010) *Crawling from the Wreckage*. Toronto, ON: Random House.

Egale Canada (2011) *Every Class in Every School*; available at archive.egale.ca/index.asp?lang=E&menu=4&item=1489

Eliot, Lise (2009) *Pink Brain, Blue Brain: how small differences grow into troublesome gaps – and what we can do about it*. New York, NY: Houghton Mifflin Harcourt Publishing Company.

Gabler, Neal "The Elusive Big Idea," *New York Times*, August 21, 2011.

Gladwell, Malcolm (2011) *Outliers: The story of success*. New York, NY: Bark Bay Books/Little, Brown and Company, Hachette Book Group.

Gottlieb, Lori, "How To Land Your Kid In Therapy" *The Atlantic*, July/August 2011, 308/1: 72.

"Harper's Index" *Harper's*, February 2011, 324/1941.

"Harper's Index" *Harper's*, October 2011, 323/1937.

Hedges, Chris (2009) *Empire of Illusion: the end of literacy and the triumph of spectacle.* New York, NY: Alfred A. Knopf.

Journal of Adolescent Health (2006) "Bullying and Suicidal Behaviors Among Urban High School Youth"; available at http://www.jahonline.org/article/S1054-139X(11)00677-X/abstract

Kahneman, Daniel (2011) *Thinking, Fast and Slow.* Toronto, ON: Doubleday Canada.

Kaiser Family Foundation (2010) "Generation M2: Media in the lives of 8- to 18-year-olds"; available at http://www.kff.org/entmedia/mh012010pkg.cfm

Kane, Jonathan and Metz, Janet, *Scientific American*, January 2012, 306, 1.

Kohn, Alfie (2011) *Feel-Bad Education and Other Contrarian Essays on Children and Schooling.* Boston, MA: Beacon Press.

Kohn, Alfie (2000) *The Case Against Standardized Testing: Raising the scores, ruining the Schools.* Portsmouth, NH: Heinemann.

Levitt, Steven D. and Dubner, Stephen J. (2006) *Freakonomics: A Rogue Economist Explores the Hidden Side of Everything.* New York, NY: HarperCollins Publishers.

Li, Anita, "South Korea cracks down on cramming" *Toronto Star*, October 7, 2011.

Loban, Walter (1976) *Language Deveopment: Kindergarten through grade twelve.* Urbana, IL: National Council of Teachers of English.

Mitchell, Alanna, "The Atkinson Series: Brainstorm, Equal at Birth" *Toronto Star*, November 3, 2009.

Namie, Gary and Ruth (2003) *The Bully At Work.* Naperville, IL: Sourcebooks.

New York Times "Technology Can Wait," October 23, 2011.

Parsons, Les (2005) *Bullied Teacher: Bullied Student (How to recognize the bullying culture in your school and what to do about it).* Markham, ON: Pembroke Publishers Ltd.

Parsons, Les (2001) *Response Journals Revisited: Maximizing learning through reading, writing, viewing, discussing, and thinking.* Markham, ON: Pembroke Publishers Ltd.

Patil, Anita, "The Great Rush Forward," *New York Times*, March 13, 2011.

Pew Research Centerr (2009) "Teens and Sexting" Internet and American Life Project; at http://pewresearch.org/pubs/1440/teens-sexting-text-messages

Ravitch, Diane (2010) *The Death and Life of the Great American School System: How testing and choice are undermining education.* New York, NY: Basic Books.

Ravitch, Diane "Schools We Can Envy" New York Review of Books, March 8, 2012.

Sacks, Peter (1999) *Standardized Minds: The high price of America's testing culture and what we can do to change it.* New York, NY: Da Cao Press.

Sahlberg, Pasi (2012) *Finnish Lessons: What can the world learn from educational change in Finland?* New York, NY: Teachers College Press.

Salutin, Rick "Why Teachers Matter" *Toronto Star*, March 26, 2011.

Scientific American, January 2012, 306, 1.

Toronto Star, August 25, 2009.

Toronto Star, "Georgia Schools Caught in Cheating Scandal" July 8, 2011.

Toronto Star, August 11, 2011.

Wiseman, Rosalind (2003) *Queen Bees and Wannabes: Helping your daughter survive cliques, gossip, boyfriends, and other realities of adolescence.* New York, NY: Three Rivers Press.

INDEX